I0955422

Advance praise for *Caring for Creation*

"In *Laudato Si'*, Pope Francis shows how we need to listen, observe and engage everything that makes up our common home, not only with the intelligence of the market, profit, and gains; but also with the intelligence of the heart, solidarity, compassion, and care, especially towards the weak and poor."

—CARDINAL PETER K.A. TURKSON,
president, Vatican Pontifical Council for Justice and Peace

"It is impossible to overstate the power of the pope's words on creation and its care, in the landmark *Laudato Si'* and elsewhere. As this volume illustrates, he has put the full power of his papacy behind the most crucial challenge we've ever faced: slowing the ongoing and horrific overheating of the planet we were given to care for."

—BILL MCKIBBEN,
author, environmentalist, founder 350.org

"These words, this message, this prophetic call from Pope Francis, are deeply inspiring and worth our reflection and serious consideration. I want to hear this message fully and take it to heart, and I urge others to do so, too, that we might all do what we can to help end environmental destruction and create a more nonviolent world."

—REV. JOHN DEAR,
author, activist, Nobel Peace Prize nominee, cofounder
CampaignNonviolence.org

"Meditate with Pope Francis on human dignity and the common good—what he calls "integral human ecology." Rejecting a "throwaway" attitude that only destroys, Pope Francis begins with praise to God our Creator (*Laudato Si'*) for the precious gift of each person and all creation. With humble joy, we seek to follow his call to cherish every person and the earth we call home."

—MOST REVEREND JOSEPH E. KURTZ, DD,
archbishop of Louisville,
president, US Conference of Catholic Bishops

"This presentation of the inspiring words of Pope Francis on the gift of creation and our abiding responsibility to care for and cultivate our common home is a rich tapestry that weaves together threads from the multiple occasions when he has addressed this priority. By listening to creation, the Creator, and one another, we are invited to contemplate and build on the interconnectedness that is the foundation of an integrated ecology."

—SÉAMUS FINN, OMI,
chief of faith consistent investing, OIP Trust,
board chair, Interfaith Center on Corporate Responsibility

Caring

FOR

Creation

~~~

INSPIRING WORDS
FROM

Pope
Francis

~~~

POPE FRANCIS
EDITED BY ALICIA VON STAMWITZ

Franciscan
MEDIA
Cincinnati, Ohio

Caring for Creation is published in collaboration with the Libreria Editrice Vaticana. All excerpts © 2016 Libreria Editrice Vaticana and used by permission.

Cover and book design by Mark Sullivan
Cover image © Giampiero Sposito | Reuters

Library of Congress Cataloging-in-Publication Data
Names: Francis, Pope, 1936- | Stamwitz, Alicia von, editor.
Title: Caring for creation : inspiring words from Pope Francis
/ Pope Francis
; edited by Alicia von Stamwitz.
Description: Cincinnati : Franciscan Media, 2016.
Identifiers: LCCN 2016017332 | ISBN 9781632530608 (hardcover with dustjacket)
Subjects: LCSH: Human ecology—Religious aspects—Catholic Church—Quotations, maxims, etc. | Francis, Pope, 1936—-Quotations.
|
Ecotheology—Quotations, maxims, etc. | Catholic Church—Doctrines—Miscellanea.
Classification: LCC BX1795.H82 F728513 2016 | DDC 261.8/8—dc23
LC record available at https://lccn.loc.gov/2016017332

ISBN 978-1-63253-060-8

Published by Franciscan Media
28 W. Liberty St.
Cincinnati, OH 45202
www.FranciscanMedia.org

Printed in the United States of America.
Printed on acid-free paper.

16 17 18 19 20 5 4 3 2 1

Contents

INTRODUCTION

All-powerful God, you are present in the whole universe and in the smallest of your creatures. You embrace with your tenderness all that exists. Pour out upon us the power of your love, that we may protect life and beauty.

—POPE FRANCIS, "A PRAYER FOR THE EARTH"

Since his inaugural Mass in March 2013, Pope Francis has frequently reminded a global audience that care for creation is among his highest priorities. In June 2015, he released his long-awaited encyclical on the environment, *Laudato Si'* (Praise Be to You), addressing it to "every person living on this planet." Named after a canticle by St. Francis of Assisi, the encyclical pairs religious insights with scientific facts to spotlight the gravity of the environmental crisis.

As a world leader with a background in science who heads a two-thousand-year-old Church, the pope is uniquely qualified to articulate a compelling vision and mission for the future. The writings, homilies, prayers, talks, and even tweets of Pope Francis in this book gather his most important and inspiring words about our shared responsibility to protect, nurture, and care for "our common home."

The planet is in peril, the pope is telling us, along with the well-being of the poor who depend on the earth's natural resources. He chastises world leaders and challenges ordinary people, reminding us that our foolish actions and careless decisions are placing lives at risk. He decries our current assaults on the natural environment and warns of the consequences of climate change.

Still, Pope Francis's message is always ultimately one of hope. In *Caring for Creation*, Pope Francis's words reveal that he believes we can move towards a new kind of conversion—a higher level of consciousness, action, and advocacy that will spark "a bold cultural revolution."

—*Alicia von Stamwitz, editor*

CHAPTER ONE

~ God's Loving Plan for Creation ~

CONTEMPLATE THE GOODNESS OF CREATION

In the first chapter of Genesis, right at the beginning of the Bible, what is emphasized is that God is pleased with his creation, stressing repeatedly the beauty and goodness of every single thing. At the end of each day, it is written: "God saw that it was good" (1:12, 18, 21, 25). If God sees creation as good, as a beautiful thing, then we too must take this attitude and see that creation is a good and beautiful thing. Now, this is the gift of knowledge that allows us to see this beauty, therefore we praise God, giving thanks to him for having granted us so much beauty. And when God finished creating man, he didn't say, "He saw that this was good," but said that this was "very good" (v. 31). In the eyes of God, we are the most beautiful thing, the greatest, the best of creation: even the angels are beneath us, we are more than the angels, as we heard in the Book of Psalms. The Lord favors us!…

All this is a source of serenity and peace and makes the Christian a joyful witness of God, in the footsteps of St. Francis of Assisi and so many saints who knew how to praise and laud his love through the contemplation of creation.

GENERAL AUDIENCE, ST. PETER'S SQUARE
WEDNESDAY, MAY 21, 2014

GOD FILLS ALL THINGS

The universe unfolds in God, who fills it completely. Hence, there is a mystical meaning to be found in a leaf, in a mountain trail, in a dewdrop, in a poor person's face. The ideal is not only to pass from the exterior to the interior to discover the action of God in the soul, but also to discover God in all things.

ENCYCLICAL LETTER, *LAUDATO SI'*, 233
SUNDAY, MAY 24, 2015

Pope Francis @Pontifex · June 18, 2015

Every creature is the object of the Father's tenderness, who gives it its place in the world.

WHY GOD CREATED THE WORLD

A young person once asked me—you know how young people ask hard questions!—"Father, what did God do before he created the world?" Believe me, I had a hard time answering that one. I told him what I am going to tell you now. Before he created the world, God was in love, because God is love. The love he had within himself, the love between the Father and the Son, in the Holy Spirit, was so great, so overflowing—I'm not sure if this is theologically precise, but you will get what I am saying— that love was so great that God could not be selfish. He had to go out from himself in order to have someone to love outside of himself. So God created the world. God made this wonderful world in which we live and which, since we are not too smart, we are now in the process of destroying.

PRAYER VIGIL FOR THE FESTIVAL OF FAMILIES,
PHILADELPHIA
SATURDAY, SEPTEMBER 26, 2015

THE EARTH, OUR BEAUTIFUL MOTHER

"*Laudato Si'*, mi' Signore"—"Praise be to you, my Lord." In the words of this beautiful canticle, St. Francis of Assisi reminds us that our common home is like a sister with whom we share our life and a beautiful mother who opens her arms to embrace us. "Praise be to you, my Lord, through our Sister, Mother Earth, who sustains and governs us, and who produces various fruit with colored flowers and herbs."

This sister now cries out to us because of the harm we have inflicted on her by our irresponsible use and abuse of the goods with which God has endowed her.

ENCYCLICAL LETTER, *LAUDATO SI'*, 1–2
SUNDAY, MAY 24, 2015

Pope Francis @Pontifex · Feb 15, 2016

Among the poor being treated worst is our planet. We cannot pretend all is fine in the face of the great environmental crisis.

THE "GRAMMAR" INSCRIBED IN NATURE

The human family has received from the Creator a common gift: nature. The Christian view of creation includes a positive judgment about the legitimacy of interventions on nature if these are meant to be beneficial and are performed responsibly; that is to say, by acknowledging the "grammar" inscribed in nature and by wisely using resources for the benefit of all, with respect for the beauty, finality and usefulness of every living being and its place in the ecosystem.

Nature, in a word, is at our disposition and we are called to exercise a responsible stewardship over it. Yet so often we are driven by greed and by the arrogance of dominion, possession, manipulation and exploitation; we do not preserve nature; nor do we respect it or consider it a gracious gift which we must care for and set at the service of our brothers and sisters, including future generations.

MESSAGE FOR 2014 WORLD DAY OF PEACE,
FROM THE VATICAN
SUNDAY, DECEMBER 8, 2013

A REALITY ILLUMINATED BY LOVE

In the Judaeo-Christian tradition, the word "creation" has a broader meaning than "nature," for it has to do with God's loving plan in which every creature has its own value and significance. Nature is usually seen as a system which can be studied, understood and controlled, whereas creation can only be understood as a gift from the outstretched hand of the Father of all, and as a reality illuminated by the love which calls us together into universal communion.

ENCYCLICAL LETTER, *LAUDATO SI'*, 76
SUNDAY, MAY 24, 2015

Pope Francis @Pontifex · June 18, 2015

"Creation" has a broader meaning than "nature"; it has to do with God's loving plan. #LaudatoSi

CREATION IS A GIFT TO BE SHARED

God does not only give us life: he gives us the Earth, he gives us all of creation. He does not only give man a partner and endless possibilities: he also gives human beings a task, he gives them a mission. He invites them to be a part of his creative work and he says: Cultivate it! I am giving you seeds, soil, water and sun. I am giving you your hands and those of your brothers and sisters. There it is, it is yours. It is a gift, a present, an offering. It is not something that can be bought or acquired. It precedes us and it will be there long after us.

Our world is a gift given to us by God so that, with him, we can make it our own. God did not will creation for himself so he could see himself reflected in it. On the contrary: creation is a gift to be shared. It is the space that God gives us to build up with one another, to build a "we." The world, history, all of time—this is the setting in which we build this "we" with God, with others, with the earth. This invitation is always present, more or less consciously in our life; it is always there.

But there is something else which is special. As Genesis recounts, after the word "cultivate," another word immediately follows: "care." Each explains the other. They go hand in hand. Those who do not cultivate do not care; those who do not care do not cultivate.

ADDRESS TO EDUCATORS, PONTIFICAL CATHOLIC
UNIVERSITY OF ECUADOR, QUITO
TUESDAY, JULY 7, 2015

Pope Francis @Pontifex · January 8, 2016

When the world slumbers in comfort and selfishness, our Christian mission is to help it rouse from sleep.

CUSTODIANS OF GOD'S GIFT

Creation is not some possession that we can lord over for our own pleasure; nor, even less, is it the property of only some people, the few. Creation is a gift, it is the marvelous gift that God has given us, so that we will take care of it and harness it for the benefit of all, always with great respect and gratitude....

We must protect creation, for it is a gift which the Lord has given us, it is God's present to us; we are the guardians of creation. When we exploit creation, we destroy that sign of God's love. To destroy creation is to say to God: "I don't care." And this is not good: this is sin.

Custody of creation is precisely custody of God's gift and it is saying to God: "Thank you, I am the guardian of creation so as to make it progress, never to destroy your gift." This must be our attitude to creation: guard it—for if we destroy creation, creation will destroy us!

GENERAL AUDIENCE, ST. PETER'S SQUARE
WEDNESDAY, MAY 21, 2014

A SIGN OF GOD'S BOUNDLESS AFFECTION

The entire material universe speaks of God's love, his boundless affection for us. Soil, water, mountains: everything is, as it were, a caress of God. The history of our friendship with God is always linked to particular places which take on an intensely personal meaning; we all remember places, and revisiting those memories does us much good. Anyone who has grown up in the hills or used to sit by the spring to drink, or played outdoors in the neighborhood square; going back to these places is a chance to recover something of their true selves.

ENCYCLICAL LETTER, *LAUDATO SI'*, 84
SUNDAY, MAY 24, 2015

ECOLOGY HAS A MORAL DIMENSION

Our time cannot ignore the issue of ecology, which is vital to man's survival, nor reduce it to merely a political question: indeed, it has a moral dimension that affects everyone, such that no one can ignore it. As disciples of Christ, we have a further reason to join with all men and women of good will to protect and defend nature and the environment. Creation is, in fact, a gift entrusted to us from the hands of the Creator.

ADDRESS TO THE ITALIAN CATHOLIC SCOUT MOVEMENT
FOR ADULTS (MASCI), PAUL VI AUDIENCE HALL
SATURDAY, NOVEMBER 8, 2014

Pope Francis @Pontifex · December 11, 2014

Ecology is essential for the survival of mankind; it is a moral issue which affects all of us.

THE GRANDEUR OF THE COSMOS

When our eyes are illumined by the Spirit, they open to contemplate God, in the beauty of nature and in the grandeur of the cosmos, and they lead us to discover how everything speaks to us about him and his love. All of this arouses in us great wonder and a profound sense of gratitude! It is the sensation we experience when we admire a work of art or any marvel whatsoever that is borne of the genius and creativity of man: before all this, the Spirit leads us to praise the Lord from the depths of our heart and to recognize, in all that we have and all that we are, an invaluable gift of God and a sign of his infinite love for us.

GENERAL AUDIENCE, ST. PETER'S SQUARE
WEDNESDAY, MAY 21, 2014

LIFT UP YOUR EYES

The Lord was able to invite others to be attentive to the beauty that there is in the world because he himself was in constant touch with nature, lending it an attention full of fondness and wonder. As he made his way throughout the land, he often stopped to contemplate the beauty sown by his Father, and invited his disciples to perceive a divine message in things: "Lift up your eyes, and see how the fields are already white for harvest" (John 4:35). "The kingdom of God is like a grain of mustard seed which a man took and sowed in his field; it is the smallest of all seeds, but once it has grown, it is the greatest of plants" (Matthew 13:31–32).

Jesus lived in full harmony with creation, and others were amazed: "What sort of man is this, that even the winds and the sea obey him?" (Matthew 8:27).

ENCYCLICAL LETTER, *LAUDATO SI'*, 97–98
SUNDAY, MAY 24, 2015

TILL AND KEEP THE EARTH

When we talk about the environment, about creation, my thoughts go to the first pages of the Bible, to the book of Genesis, where it says that God puts men and women on the earth to till it and keep it (cf. 2:15). And these questions occur to me: What does cultivating and preserving the earth mean? Are we truly cultivating and caring for creation? Or are we exploiting and neglecting it? The verb "cultivate" reminds me of the care a farmer takes to ensure that his land will be productive and that his produce will be shared.

What great attention, enthusiasm and dedication! Cultivating and caring for creation is an instruction of God which he gave not only at the beginning of history, but has also given to each one of us; it is part of his plan; it means making the world increase with responsibility, transforming it so that it may be a garden, an inhabitable place for us all.

GENERAL AUDIENCE, ST. PETER'S SQUARE
WEDNESDAY, JUNE 5, 2013

THE WORLD IS A JOYFUL MYSTERY

I am pleased to be here, in this country of singular beauty, blessed by God in its diverse regions: its Altiplano and valleys, its Amazon region, its deserts and the incomparable lakes. The preamble of your Constitution gives poetic expression to this natural beauty: "In ancient times the mountains arose, rivers changed course and lakes were formed. Our Amazonia, our wetlands and our highlands, and our plains and valleys were decked with greenery and flowers." It makes me realize once again that "rather than a problem to be solved, the world is a joyful mystery to be contemplated with gladness and praise" (*Laudato Si'*, 12).

WELCOME CEREMONY, AIRPORT "EL ALTO,"
LA PAZ, BOLIVIA
WEDNESDAY, JULY 8, 2015

Pope Francis @Pontifex · June 5, 2013
Care of creation is not just something God spoke of at the dawn of history: he entrusts it to each of us as part of his plan.

EVOLUTION IN NATURE

When we read the account of creation in Genesis we risk imagining that God was a magician, complete with an all-powerful magic wand. But that was not so. He created beings and he let them develop according to the internal laws with which he endowed each one, that they might develop and reach their fullness. He gave autonomy to the beings of the universe at the same time in which he assured them of his continual presence, giving life to every reality.... The beginning of the world was not a work of chaos that owes its origin to another, but derives directly from a supreme Principle who creates out of love. The Big Bang theory, which is proposed today as the origin of the world, does not contradict the intervention of a divine Creator but depends on it. Evolution in nature does not conflict with the notion of creation, because evolution presupposes the creation of beings who evolve.

ADDRESS, THE PONTIFICAL ACADEMY OF SCIENCES,
CASINA OF PIUS IV
MONDAY, OCTOBER 27, 2014

WORK IS PART OF GOD'S LOVING PLAN

The book of Genesis tells us that God created man and woman entrusting them with the task of filling the earth and subduing it, which does not mean exploiting it but nurturing and protecting it, caring for it through their work (cf. Genesis 1:28; 2:15). Work is part of God's loving plan; we are called to cultivate and care for all the goods of creation and in this way share in the work of creation!

GENERAL AUDIENCE, ST. PETER'S SQUARE
WEDNESDAY, MAY 1, 2013

Pope Francis @Pontifex · September 1, 2015

Today is the World Day of Prayer for the Care of Creation. Let us work and pray.

DIGNIFIED WORK AND THE
PRESERVATION OF CREATION

There is no social hope without dignified employment for all....

I said "dignified" work, and I emphasize it because unfortunately, especially when there is a crisis and the need is pressing, inhumane work increases, slave-labor, work without the proper security or respect for creation, or without respect for rest, celebrations and the family and work on Sundays when it isn't necessary. Work must be combined with the preservation of creation so that this may be responsibly safeguarded for future generations. Creation is not a good to be exploited but a gift to look after. Ecological commitment itself affords an opportunity for new concern in the sectors linked to it, such as energy, and the prevention and removal of different forms of pollution, being alert to forest fires in the wooded land that is your patrimony, and so forth. May caring for creation, and looking after man through dignified work be a common task! Ecology...and also "human ecology"!

ADDRESS TO THE WORKERS OF LARGO CARLO FELICE,
CAGLIARI
SUNDAY, SEPTEMBER 22, 2013

THREATS TO GOD'S PLAN FOR US

God chose and blessed us for a purpose: to be holy and blameless in his sight (Ephesians 1:4). He chose us, each of us to be witnesses of his truth and his justice in this world. He created the world as a beautiful garden and asked us to care for it. But through sin, man has disfigured that natural beauty; through sin, man has also destroyed the unity and beauty of our human family, creating social structures which perpetuate poverty, ignorance and corruption.

Sometimes, when we see the troubles, difficulties and wrongs all around us, we are tempted to give up. It seems that the promises of the Gospel do not apply; they are unreal. But the Bible tells us that the great threat to God's plan for us is, and always has been, the lie. The devil is the father of lies. Often he hides his snares behind the appearance of sophistication, the allure of being "modern," "like everyone else." He distracts us with the view of ephemeral pleasures, superficial pastimes. And so we squander our God-given gifts by tinkering with gadgets; we squander our money on gambling and drink; we turn in on ourselves. We forget to remain focused on the things that really matter. We forget to remain, at heart, children of God.

HOMILY, RIZAL PARK, MANILA (PHILIPPINES)
SUNDAY, JANUARY 18, 2015

THE FREEDOM TO PROTECT OUR PLANET

We must not see the Ten Commandments as limitations of freedom—no, that is not what they are—but rather as signposts to freedom. They are not restrictions but indicators of freedom. They teach us to avoid the slavery to which we are condemned by so many idols that we ourselves build—we have experimented with them so often in history, and we are still experimenting with them today. They teach us to open ourselves to a broader dimension than that of the material, and to show people respect, overcoming the greed for power, for possessions, for money, in order to be honest and sincere in our relations, to protect the whole of creation and to nourish our planet with lofty, noble spiritual ideals.

VIDEO MESSAGE, "TEN SQUARES FOR TEN
COMMANDMENTS," FROM THE VATICAN
SATURDAY, JUNE 8, 2013

Pope Francis @Pontifex · July 2, 2015

A great challenge: stop ruining the garden which God has entrusted to us so that all may enjoy it.

ST. FRANCIS'S HYMN OF PRAISE

When we can see God reflected in all that exists, our hearts are moved to praise the Lord for all his creatures and to worship him in union with them. This sentiment finds magnificent expression in the hymn of St. Francis of Assisi:

> Praised be you, my Lord, with all your creatures,
> especially Sir Brother Sun,
> who is the day and through whom you give us
> light.
> And he is beautiful and radiant with great
> splendor;
> and bears a likeness of you, Most High.
> Praised be you, my Lord, through Sister Moon
> and the stars,
> in heaven you formed them clear and precious
> and beautiful.

Praised be you, my Lord, through Brother Wind,
and through the air, cloudy and serene, and every
kind of weather
through whom you give sustenance to your
creatures.
Praised be you, my Lord, through Sister Water,
who is very useful and humble and precious and
chaste.
Praised be you, my Lord, through Brother Fire,
through whom you light the night,
and he is beautiful and playful and robust and
strong.

ENCYCLICAL LETTER, *LAUDATO SI'*, 87
SUNDAY, MAY 24, 2015

LET US RESPECT CREATION!

St. Francis of Assisi bears witness to the need to respect all that God has created and as he created it, without manipulating and destroying creation; rather to help it grow, to become more beautiful and more like what God created it to be. And above all, St. Francis witnesses to respect for everyone, he testifies that each of us is called to protect our neighbor, that the human person is at the center of creation, at the place where God—our Creator—willed that we should be. Not at the mercy of the idols we have created! Harmony and peace! Francis was a man of harmony and peace. From this City of Peace, I repeat with all the strength and the meekness of love: Let us respect creation, let us not be instruments of destruction!

HOMILY, ST. FRANCIS SQUARE, ASSISI
FRIDAY, OCTOBER 4, 2013

NATURE, A MAGNIFICENT BOOK

St. Francis, faithful to Scripture, invites us to see nature as a magnificent book in which God speaks to us and grants us a glimpse of his infinite beauty and goodness. "Through the greatness and the beauty of creatures one comes to know by analogy their maker" (Wisdom 13:5); indeed, "his eternal power and divinity have been made known through his works since the creation of the world" (Romans 1:20). For this reason, Francis asked that part of the friary garden always be left untouched, so that wild flowers and herbs could grow there, and those who saw them could raise their minds to God, the Creator of such beauty. Rather than a problem to be solved, the world is a joyful mystery to be contemplated with gladness and praise.

ENCYCLICAL LETTER, *LAUDATO SI'*, 12
SUNDAY, MAY 24, 2015

THE MAN WHO LOVES
AND PROTECTS CREATION

Some people wanted to know why the Bishop of Rome wished to be called Francis. Some thought of Francis Xavier, Francis De Sales, and also Francis of Assisi. I will tell you the story. During the election, I was seated next to the Archbishop Emeritus of São Paolo and Prefect Emeritus of the Congregation for the Clergy, Cardinal Claudio Hummes: a good friend, a good friend! When things were looking dangerous, he encouraged me. And when the votes reached two thirds, there was the usual applause, because the Pope had been elected. And he gave me a hug and a kiss, and said: "Don't forget the poor!" And those words came to me: the poor, the poor. Then, right away, thinking of the poor, I thought of Francis of Assisi. Then I thought of all the wars, as the votes were still being counted, till the end. Francis is also the man of peace. That is how the name came into my heart: Francis of Assisi. For me, he is the man of poverty, the man of peace, the man who loves and protects creation; these days we do not have a very good relationship with creation, do we?

ADDRESS TO REPRESENTATIVES OF THE
COMMUNICATIONS MEDIA, PAUL VI AUDIENCE HALL
SATURDAY, MARCH 16, 2013

MINDSET INFLUENCES BEHAVIOR

By learning to see and appreciate beauty, we learn to reject self-interested pragmatism. If someone has not learned to stop and admire something beautiful, we should not be surprised if he or she treats everything as an object to be used and abused without scruple. If we want to bring about deep change, we need to realize that certain mindsets really do influence our behavior. Our efforts at education will be inadequate and ineffectual unless we strive to promote a new way of thinking about human beings, life, society and our relationship with nature.

ENCYCLICAL LETTER, *LAUDATO SI'*, 215
SUNDAY, MAY 24, 2015

Pope Francis @Pontifex · June 19, 2015

The teachings of the Gospel have direct consequences for our way of thinking, feeling and living. #LaudatoSi

THE GIFT ENTRUSTED TO US

It is our profound conviction that the future of the human family depends also on how we safeguard—both prudently and compassionately, with justice and fairness—the gift of creation that our Creator has entrusted to us. Therefore, we acknowledge in repentance the wrongful mistreatment of our planet, which is tantamount to sin before the eyes of God. We reaffirm our responsibility and obligation to foster a sense of humility and moderation so that all may feel the need to respect creation and to safeguard it with care. Together, we pledge our commitment to raising awareness about the stewardship of creation; we appeal to all people of goodwill to consider ways of living less wastefully and more frugally, manifesting less greed and more generosity for the protection of God's world and the benefit of His people.

COMMON DECLARATION OF POPE FRANCIS AND THE
ECUMENICAL PATRIARCH BARTHOLOMEW I, JERUSALEM
SUNDAY, MAY 25, 2014

AN INVITATION TO ALL

This is the invitation which I address to everyone: Let us accept the grace of Christ's Resurrection! Let us be renewed by God's mercy, let us be loved by Jesus, let us enable the power of his love to transform our lives too; and let us become agents of this mercy, channels through which God can water the earth, protect all creation and make justice and peace flourish.

URBI ET ORBI, LOGGIA OF ST. PETER'S BASILICA
EASTER SUNDAY, MARCH 31, 2013

Pope Francis @Pontifex · April 30, 2014

Let us put our trust in God's power at work! With him, we can do great things. He will give us the joy of being his disciples.

TAKE CARE OF GOD'S BEAUTIFUL GIFTS

Once I was in the countryside and I heard a saying from a simple person who had a great love for flowers and took care of them. He said to me: "We must take care of the beautiful things that God has given us! Creation is ours so that we can receive good things from it; not exploit it, to protect it. God forgives always, we men forgive sometimes, but creation never forgives and if you don't care for it, it will destroy you."

This should make us think and should make us ask the Holy Spirit for the gift of knowledge in order to understand better that creation is a most beautiful gift of God.

GENERAL AUDIENCE, ST. PETER'S SQUARE
WEDNESDAY, MAY 21, 2014

Pope Francis @Pontifex · March 19, 2013
Let us keep a place for Christ in our lives, let us care for one another and let us be loving custodians of creation.

THIS IS THE KINGDOM OF GOD!

When a person discovers God, the true treasure, he abandons a selfish lifestyle and seeks to share with others the charity which comes from God. He who becomes a friend of God loves his brothers and sisters, commits himself to safeguarding their life and their health, and also to respecting the environment and nature. I know that you suffer because of these things. Today, when I arrived, one of you approached me and told me: Father, give us hope! But I cannot give you hope, I can tell you that where Jesus is, there is hope; where Jesus is, there is love for brothers and sisters, there is the commitment to safeguarding their life and their health and to respecting the environment and nature. This is the hope that never disappoints, the hope which Jesus gives!…

The Lord says: it is not important to me that you do this or that; it is important to me that the orphan is cared for, that the widow is cared for, that the outcast person is heard, that creation is protected. This is the Kingdom of God!

HOMILY, PARK OF THE ROYAL PALACE, CASERTA
SATURDAY, JULY 26, 2014

THE ILLUSION OF POWER

"Adam, where are you?" This is the first question which God asks man after his sin. "Adam, where are you?" Adam lost his bearings, his place in creation, because he thought he could be powerful, able to control everything, to be God. Harmony was lost; man erred and this error occurs over and over again also in relationships with others. "The other" is no longer a brother or sister to be loved, but simply someone who disturbs my life and my comfort. God asks a second question: "Cain, where is your brother?" The illusion of being powerful, of being as great as God, even of being God himself, leads to a whole series of errors, a chain of death, even to the spilling of a brother's blood!

God's two questions echo even today, as forcefully as ever! How many of us, myself included, have lost our bearings; we are no longer attentive to the world in which we live; we don't care; we don't protect what God created for everyone, and we end up unable even to care for one another! And when humanity as a whole loses its bearings, it results in tragedies like the one we have witnessed.

HOMILY, SALINA QUARTER, LAMPEDUSA
MONDAY, JULY 8, 2013

AUTHORITY COMES FROM GOD

Faith…by revealing the love of God the Creator, enables us to respect nature all the more, and to discern in it a grammar written by the hand of God and a dwelling place entrusted to our protection and care. Faith also helps us to devise models of development which are based not simply on utility and profit, but consider creation as a gift for which we are all indebted; it teaches us to create just forms of government, in the realization that authority comes from God and is meant for the service of the common good.

ENCYCLICAL LETTER, *LUMEN FIDEI*, 55
SATURDAY, JUNE 29, 2013

Pope Francis @Pontifex · May 8, 2013

I have come that they may have life and have it in abundance, says Jesus. This is where true wealth is found, not in material things!

A NEW EARTH

The Conciliar Constitution *Gaudium et Spes*, faced with these questions that forever resonate in the hearts of men and women, states: "We do not know the time for the consummation of the earth and of humanity, nor do we know how all things will be transformed. As deformed by sin, the shape of this world will pass away; but we are taught that God is preparing a new dwelling place and a new earth where justice will abide, and whose blessedness will answer and surpass all the longings for peace which spring up in the human heart" (n. 39)....

At the same time, Sacred Scripture teaches us that the fulfillment of this marvelous plan cannot but involve everything that surrounds us and came from the heart and mind of God. The Apostle Paul says it explicitly, when he says that "Creation itself will be set free from its bondage to decay and obtain the glorious liberty of the children of God" (Romans 8:21). Other texts utilize the image of a "new heaven" and a "new earth" (cf. 2 Peter 3:13;

Revelations 21:1), in the sense that the whole universe will be renewed and will be freed once and for all from every trace of evil and from death itself. What lies ahead is the fulfillment of a transformation that in reality is already happening, beginning with the death and resurrection of Christ. Hence, it is the new creation; it is not, therefore, the annihilation of the cosmos and of everything around us, but the bringing of all things into the fullness of being, of truth and of beauty. This is the design that God, the Father, Son and Holy Spirit, willed from eternity to realize and is realizing.

GENERAL AUDIENCE, ST. PETER'S SQUARE
WEDNESDAY, NOVEMBER 26, 2014

Pope Francis @Pontifex · June 18, 2015
The world we have received also belongs to who will follow us. #LaudatoSi

EACH DAY, BEAUTY IS BORN ANEW

Christ's resurrection is not an event of the past; it contains a vital power which has permeated this world. Where all seems to be dead, signs of the resurrection suddenly spring up. It is an irresistible force. Often it seems that God does not exist: all around us we see persistent injustice, evil, indifference and cruelty. But it is also true that in the midst of darkness something new always springs to life and sooner or later produces fruit. On razed land life breaks through, stubbornly yet invincibly. However dark things are, goodness always reemerges and spreads. Each day in our world, beauty is born anew, it rises transformed through the storms of history. Values always tend to reappear under new guises, and human beings have arisen time after time from situations that seemed doomed. Such is the power of the resurrection, and all who evangelize are instruments of that power.

APOSTOLIC EXHORTATION, *EVANGELII GAUDIUM*, 276
SUNDAY, NOVEMBER 24, 2013

THE WAY FORWARD

What should our attitude be if we want to be part of this multitude journeying to the Father, in this world of devastation, in this world of war, in this world of tribulation? Our attitude, as we heard in the Gospel, is the attitude of the Beatitudes. That path alone will lead us to the encounter with God. That path alone will save us from destruction, from destroying the earth, creation, morality, history, family, everything. That path alone. But it too will bring us through bad things! It will bring us problems, persecution. And so, these people who are suffering so much today because of the selfishness of destroyers, of our brothers' destroyers, these people struggle onwards with the Beatitudes, with the hope of finding God, of coming face-to-face with the Lord, in the hope of becoming saints at the moment of our final encounter with Him.

May the Lord help us and give us the grace of this hope, but also the grace of courage to emerge from all this destruction, devastation, the relativism of life, the exclusion of others, exclusion of values, exclusion of all that the Lord has given us: the exclusion of peace.

HOMILY, SOLEMNITY OF ALL SAINTS,
CEMETERY OF VERANO
SATURDAY, NOVEMBER 1, 2014

CHAPTER TWO

~ Everything Is Connected ~

A LIVING NETWORK

It cannot be emphasized enough how everything is interconnected. Time and space are not independent of one another, and not even atoms or subatomic particles can be considered in isolation. Just as the different aspects of the planet—physical, chemical and biological—are interrelated, so too living species are part of a network which we will never fully explore and understand. A good part of our genetic code is shared by many living beings.

ENCYCLICAL LETTER, *LAUDATO SI'*, 138
SUNDAY, MAY 24, 2015

Pope Francis @Pontifex · June 18, 2015
Interdependence obliges us to think of one world with a common plan.

ANY HARM TO THE ENVIRONMENT IS A HARM TO HUMANITY

Any harm done to the environment…is harm done to humanity…because every creature, particularly a living creature, has an intrinsic value, in its existence, its life, its beauty and its interdependence with other creatures. We Christians, together with the other monotheistic religions, believe that the universe is the fruit of a loving decision by the Creator, who permits man respectfully to use creation for the good of his fellow men and for the glory of the Creator; he is not authorized to abuse it, much less to destroy it. In all religions, the environment is a fundamental good.

ADDRESS TO THE GENERAL ASSEMBLY OF THE UNITED NATIONS, UNITED NATIONS HEADQUARTERS, NEW YORK FRIDAY, SEPTEMBER 25, 2015

THREE VITAL RELATIONSHIPS

The creation accounts in the book of Genesis contain, in their own symbolic and narrative language, profound teachings about human existence and its historical reality. They suggest that human life is grounded in three fundamental and closely intertwined relationships: with God, with our neighbor and with the earth itself. According to the Bible, these three vital relationships have been broken, both outwardly and within us. This rupture is sin. The harmony between the Creator, humanity and creation as a whole was disrupted by our presuming to take the place of God and refusing to acknowledge our creaturely limitations. This in turn distorted our mandate to "have dominion" over the earth (cf. Genesis 1:28), to "till it and keep it" (Genesis 2:15). As a result, the originally harmonious relationship between human beings and nature became conflictual (cf. Genesis 3:17–19). It is significant that the harmony which St. Francis of Assisi experienced with all creatures was seen as a healing of that rupture.

ENCYCLICAL LETTER, *LAUDATO SI'*, 66
SUNDAY, MAY 24, 2015

THE PATRON SAINT OF INTEGRAL ECOLOGY

I believe that St. Francis is the example par excellence of care for the vulnerable and of an integral ecology lived out joyfully and authentically. He is the patron saint of all who study and work in the area of ecology, and he is also much loved by non-Christians. He was particularly concerned for God's creation and for the poor and outcast. He loved, and was deeply loved for his joy, his generous self-giving, his openheartedness. He was a mystic and a pilgrim who lived in simplicity and in wonderful harmony with God, with others, with nature and with himself. He shows us just how inseparable the bond is between concern for nature, justice for the poor, commitment to society, and interior peace.

ENCYCLICAL LETTER, *LAUDATO SI'*, 10
SUNDAY, MAY 24, 2015

Pope Francis @Pontifex · June 18, 2015
We need an integrated approach to combating poverty and protecting nature.

A HARMONIOUS UNITY

Our world, in the heart and mind of God, is the "house of harmony and peace,"…it is the space in which everyone is able to find their proper place and feel "at home," because it is "good." All of creation forms a harmonious and good unity, but above all humanity, made in the image and likeness of God, is one family, in which relationships are marked by a true fraternity not only in words: the other person is a brother or sister to love, and our relationship with God, who is love, fidelity and goodness, mirrors every human relationship and brings harmony to the whole of creation.

VIGIL OF PRAYER FOR PEACE, ST. PETER'S SQUARE
SATURDAY, SEPTEMBER 7, 2013

EVERYTHING IS INTERRELATED

Because we dwell in a common home, we cannot help but ask ourselves about the state of its health, as I sought to do in *Laudato Si'*. Water and air pollution, the indiscriminate exploitation of forests, and the destruction of the natural environment are often the result of man's indifference to man, since everything is interrelated. Then too, there is the way we treat animals, which has an effect on the way we treat other people, not to mention what people freely do elsewhere that they would never dare do at home.

In these and in other situations, indifference leads to self-absorption and a lack of commitment. It thus contributes to the absence of peace with God, with our neighbor and with the environment.

MESSAGE FOR THE 2016 WORLD DAY OF PEACE,
FROM THE VATICAN
SUNDAY, DECEMBER 8, 2015

THE GOOD FUNCTIONING
OF THE ECOSYSTEM

It is not enough, however, to think of different species merely as potential "resources" to be exploited, while overlooking the fact that they have value in themselves. Each year sees the disappearance of thousands of plant and animal species which we will never know, which our children will never see, because they have been lost forever. The great majority become extinct for reasons related to human activity. Because of us, thousands of species will no longer give glory to God by their very existence, nor convey their message to us. We have no such right.

It may well disturb us to learn of the extinction of mammals or birds, since they are more visible. But the good functioning of ecosystems also requires fungi, algae, worms, insects, reptiles and an innumerable variety of microorganisms. Some less numerous species, although generally unseen, nonetheless play a critical role in maintaining the equilibrium of a particular place.

ENCYCLICAL LETTER, *LAUDATO SI'*, 33–34
SUNDAY, MAY 24, 2015

THE COMMON GOOD MUST BE
A PRIMARY GOAL

The grave environmental crisis facing our world demands an ever greater sensitivity to the relationship between human beings and nature. We have a responsibility to pass on the beauty of nature in its integrity to future generations and an obligation to exercise a just stewardship of the gifts we have received....

In effect, there is a clear link between the protection of nature and the building of a just and equitable social order. There can be no renewal of our relationship with nature, without a renewal of humanity itself (cf. *Laudato Si'*, 118). To the extent that our societies experience divisions, whether ethnic, religious or economic, all men and women of good will are called to work for reconciliation and peace, forgiveness and healing. In the work of building a sound democratic order, strengthening cohesion and integration, tolerance and respect for others, the pursuit of the common good must be a primary goal.

ADDRESS TO AUTHORITIES AND THE DIPLOMATIC
CORPS, STATE HOUSE, NAIROBI (KENYA)
WEDNESDAY, NOVEMBER 25, 2015

THE POOR SUFFER THE MOST

The human environment and the natural environment deteriorate together; we cannot adequately combat environmental degradation unless we attend to causes related to human and social degradation. In fact, the deterioration of the environment and of society affects the most vulnerable people on the planet.... For example, the depletion of fishing reserves especially hurts small fishing communities without the means to replace those resources; water pollution particularly affects the poor, who cannot buy bottled water; and rises in the sea level mainly affect impoverished coastal populations who have nowhere else to go.

ENCYCLICAL LETTER, *LAUDATO SI'*, 48
SUNDAY, MAY 24, 2015

Pope Francis @Pontifex · June 18, 2015

The human environment and the natural environment deteriorate together.

A DELICATE EQUILIBRIA

This responsibility for God's earth means that human beings, endowed with intelligence, must respect the laws of nature and the delicate equilibria existing between the creatures of this world, for "he commanded and they were created; and he established them for ever and ever; he fixed their bounds and he set a law which cannot pass away" (Psalm 148:5b–6). The laws found in the Bible dwell on relationships, not only among individuals but also with other living beings. "You shall not see your brother's donkey or his ox fallen down by the way and withhold your help.... If you chance to come upon a bird's nest in any tree or on the ground, with young ones or eggs and the mother sitting upon the young or upon the eggs; you shall not take the mother with the young" (Deuteronomy 22:4, 6). Along these same lines, rest on the seventh day is meant not only for human beings, but also so "that your ox and your donkey may have rest" (Exodus 23:12). Clearly, the Bible has no place for a tyrannical anthropocentrism unconcerned for other creatures.

ENCYCLICAL LETTER, *LAUDATO SI'*, 68
SUNDAY, MAY 24, 2015

A RADICAL COMMUNION WITH NATURE

[St.] Francis helps us to see that an integral ecology calls for openness to categories which transcend the language of mathematics and biology and take us to the heart of what it is to be human. Just as happens when we fall in love with someone, whenever he would gaze at the sun, the moon or the smallest of animals, he burst into song, drawing all other creatures into his praise. He communed with all creation, even preaching to the flowers, inviting them "to praise the Lord, just as if they were endowed with reason." His response to the world around him was so much more than intellectual appreciation or economic calculus, for to him each and every creature was a sister united to him by bonds of affection. That is why he felt called to care for all that exists.... The poverty and austerity of St. Francis were no mere veneer of asceticism, but something much more radical: a refusal to turn reality into an object simply to be used and controlled.

ENCYCLICAL LETTER, *LAUDATO SI'*, 11
SUNDAY, MAY 24, 2015

Pope Francis @Pontifex · June 18, 2015

It is contrary to human dignity to cause animals to suffer or die needlessly. #LaudatoSi

THE IMPRINT OF THE CREATOR

All of nature that surrounds us is created like us, created together with us, and in a common destiny it tends to find its fulfillment and ultimate end in God himself—the Bible says "new heavens and a new earth" (cf. Isaiah 65:17, 2 Peter 3:13; Revelations 21:1). This doctrine of our faith is an even stronger stimulus for us to have a responsible and respectful relationship with creation: in inanimate nature, in plants and in animals, we recognize the imprint of the Creator, and in our fellow kind, His very image.

ADDRESS TO THE ITALIAN CATHOLIC SCOUT MOVEMENT
FOR ADULTS (MASCI), PAUL VI AUDIENCE HALL
SATURDAY, NOVEMBER 8, 2014

Pope Francis @Pontifex · April 21, 2015
We need to care for the earth so that it may continue, as God willed, to be a source of life for the entire human family.

THE URGENT NEED FOR A HUMAN ECOLOGY

"Cultivating and caring" do not only entail the relationship between us and the environment, between man and creation. They also concern human relations. The popes have spoken of a human ecology closely connected with environmental ecology. We are living in a time of crisis; we see it in the environment, but above all we see it in men and women. The human person is in danger: this much is certain—the human person is in danger today, hence the urgent need for a human ecology! And the peril is grave, because the cause of the problem is not superficial but deeply rooted. It is not merely a question of economics but of ethics and anthropology.

GENERAL AUDIENCE, ST. PETER'S SQUARE
WEDNESDAY, JUNE 5, 2013

WE ARE RESPONSIBLE FOR ONE ANOTHER

There has been a tragic rise in the number of migrants seeking to flee from the growing poverty caused by environmental degradation. They are not recognized by international conventions as refugees; they bear the loss of the lives they have left behind without enjoying any legal protection whatsoever. Sadly, there is widespread indifference to such suffering, which is even now taking place throughout our world. Our lack of response to these tragedies involving our brothers and sisters points to the loss of that sense of responsibility for our fellow men and women upon which all civil society is founded.

ENCYCLICAL LETTER, *LAUDATO SI'*, 25
SUNDAY, MAY 24, 2015

Pope Francis @Pontifex · June 18, 2015

We have to hear both the cry of the earth and the cry of the poor. #LaudatoSi

A CULTURE OF SOLIDARITY

A few days ago, on the Feast of Corpus Christi, we read the account of the miracle of the multiplication of the loaves. Jesus fed the multitude with five loaves and two fish. And the end of this passage is important: "And all ate and were satisfied. And they took up what was left over, twelve baskets of broken pieces" (Luke 9:17). Jesus asked the disciples to ensure that nothing was wasted: nothing thrown out! And there is this fact of twelve baskets. Why twelve? What does it mean? Twelve is the number of the tribes of Israel, it represents symbolically the whole people. And this tells us that when the food was shared fairly, with solidarity, no one was deprived of what he needed, every community could meet the needs of its poorest members. Human and environmental ecology go hand in hand.

I would therefore like us all to make the serious commitment to respect and care for creation, to pay attention to every person, to combat the culture of waste and of throwing out so as to foster a culture of solidarity and encounter. Thank you.

GENERAL AUDIENCE, ST. PETER'S SQUARE
WEDNESDAY, JUNE 5, 2013

ECOLOGICAL AND SOCIAL JUSTICE

We have to realize that a true ecological approach always becomes a social approach; it must integrate questions of justice in debates on the environment, so as to hear both the cry of the earth and the cry of the poor.

ENCYCLICAL LETTER, *LAUDATO SI'*, 49
SUNDAY, MAY 24, 2015

Pope Francis @Pontifex · June 18, 2015

The deterioration of the environment and of society affect the most vulnerable people on the planet.

WE NEED ONE ANOTHER

On the way to the Cathedral from the airport, I was able to admire the peaks of Hayna Potosí, the "young mountain," and Illimani, the mountain which shows "the place where the sun rises." I also saw the ingenious way in which many houses and neighborhoods blended with the hillsides and was struck by the architecture of some of these structures. The natural environment is closely related to the social, political and economic environment. It is urgent for all of us to lay the foundations of an integral ecology— this is a question of health—an integral ecology capable of respecting all these human dimensions in resolving the grave social and environmental issues of our time. Otherwise, the glaciers of those mountains will continue to recede, and our sense of gratitude and responsibility with regard to these gifts, our concern for the world we want to leave to future generations, for its meaning and values, will melt just like those glaciers (cf. *Laudato Si'*, 159–160). And we need be aware of this…. Because everything is related, we need one another.

MEETING WITH CIVIL AUTHORITIES,
LA PAZ CATHEDRAL, BOLIVIA
WEDNESDAY, JULY 8, 2015

A RELATIONSHIP OF MUTUAL RESPONSIBILITY

We are not God. The earth was here before us and it has been given to us.... Although it is true that we Christians have at times incorrectly interpreted the Scriptures, nowadays we must forcefully reject the notion that our being created in God's image and given dominion over the earth justifies absolute domination over other creatures. The biblical texts are to be read in their context, with an appropriate hermeneutic, recognizing that they tell us to "till and keep" the garden of the world (cf. Genesis 2:15). "Tilling" refers to cultivating, plowing or working, while "keeping" means caring, protecting, overseeing and preserving. This implies a relationship of mutual responsibility between human beings and nature. Each community can take from the bounty of the earth whatever it needs for subsistence, but it also has the duty to protect the earth and to ensure its fruitfulness for coming generations.

ENCYCLICAL LETTER, *LAUDATO SI'*, 67
SUNDAY, MAY 24, 2015

A PROPHETIC CALL

There are other weak and defenseless beings who are frequently at the mercy of economic interests or indiscriminate exploitation. I am speaking of creation as a whole. We human beings are not only the beneficiaries but also the stewards of other creatures. Thanks to our bodies, God has joined us so closely to the world around us that we can feel the desertification of the soil almost as a physical ailment, and the extinction of a species as a painful disfigurement. Let us not leave in our wake a swath of destruction and death which will affect our own lives and those of future generations.

APOSTOLIC EXHORTATION, *EVANGELII GAUDIUM*, 215
SUNDAY, NOVEMBER 24, 2013

Pope Francis @Pontifex · June 18, 2015
"To commit a crime against the natural world is a sin against ourselves and a sin against God." (Patriarch Bartholomew)

COMPASSION FOR OUR FELLOW HUMAN BEINGS

A sense of deep communion with the rest of nature cannot be real if our hearts lack tenderness, compassion and concern for our fellow human beings. It is clearly inconsistent to combat trafficking in endangered species while remaining completely indifferent to human trafficking, unconcerned about the poor, or undertaking to destroy another human being deemed unwanted. This compromises the very meaning of our struggle for the sake of the environment. It is no coincidence that, in the canticle in which St. Francis praises God for his creatures, he goes on to say: "Praised be you my Lord, through those who give pardon for your love." Everything is connected. Concern for the environment thus needs to be joined to a sincere love for our fellow human beings and an unwavering commitment to resolving the problems of society.

ENCYCLICAL LETTER, *LAUDATO SI'*, 91
SUNDAY, MAY 24, 2015

WE CANNOT POSSESS CREATION

An economic system centered on the deity money also needs to plunder nature to sustain consumption at the frenetic level it needs. Climate change, the loss of biodiversity, and deforestation are already showing their devastating effects in terrible cataclysms which we see and from which you the humble suffer most—you who live near the coast in precarious dwellings, or so economically vulnerable that you lose everything due to a natural disaster. Brothers and sisters, creation is not a possession that we can dispose of as we wish; much less is it the property of some, of only a few. Creation is a gift, it is a present, it is a marvelous gift given to us by God so that we might care for it and use it, always gratefully and always respectfully, for the benefit of everyone.

ADDRESS TO PARTICIPANTS IN THE WORLD MEETING OF
POPULAR MOVEMENTS, OLD SYNOD HALL
TUESDAY, OCTOBER 28, 2014

ONE HEART, ONE PILGRIMAGE

Our indifference or cruelty towards fellow creatures of this world sooner or later affects the treatment we mete out to other human beings. We have only one heart, and the same wretchedness which leads us to mistreat an animal will not be long in showing itself in our relationships with other people.... Everything is related, and we human beings are united as brothers and sisters on a wonderful pilgrimage, woven together by the love God has for each of his creatures and which also unites us in fond affection with Brother Sun, Sister Moon, Brother River and Mother Earth.

ENCYCLICAL LETTER, *LAUDATO SI'*, 92
SUNDAY, MAY 24, 2015

Pope Francis @Pontifex · June 19, 2015

An integral ecology includes taking time to reflect on our lifestyle and our ideals. #LaudatoSi

RESPECT FOR NATURE AND HUMAN BEINGS

It is intolerable that millions of people around the world are dying of hunger while tons of food are discarded each day from our tables. Respect for nature also calls for recognizing that man himself is a fundamental part of it. Along with an environmental ecology, there is also need of that human ecology which consists in respect for the person.

ADDRESS TO THE EUROPEAN PARLIAMENT,
STRASBOURG, FRANCE
TUESDAY, NOVEMBER 25, 2014

Pope Francis @Pontifex · October 24, 2015
Economic development needs to have a human face so that no one will be excluded.

WE MUST SEEK COMPREHENSIVE SOLUTIONS

When we speak of the "environment," what we really mean is a relationship existing between nature and the society which lives in it. Nature cannot be regarded as something separate from ourselves or as a mere setting in which we live. We are part of nature, included in it and thus in constant interaction with it. Recognizing the reasons why a given area is polluted requires a study of the workings of society, its economy, its behavior patterns, and the ways it grasps reality. Given the scale of change, it is no longer possible to find a specific, discrete answer for each part of the problem. It is essential to seek comprehensive solutions which consider the interactions within natural systems themselves and with social systems. We are faced not with two separate crises, one environmental and the other social, but rather with one complex crisis which is both social and environmental. Strategies for a solution demand an integrated approach to combating poverty, restoring dignity to the excluded, and at the same time protecting nature.

ENCYCLICAL LETTER, *LAUDATO SI'*, 139
SUNDAY, MAY 24, 2015

THE PATRIMONY OF ALL

Among the principal causes of poverty is an economic system which plunders nature—I am thinking of deforestation in particular, but also of environmental disasters and the loss of biodiversity. It bears repeating that creation is not a possession that we can dispose of as we please, much less a possession of only a few. Creation is a magnificent gift that God has given us to care for and use to the benefit of all, with respect. I encourage you, therefore, to carry on in your commitment so that creation may continue to be the patrimony of everyone, to be handed down in all its beauty to future generations.

ADDRESS TO THE FEDERATION OF CHRISTIAN
ORGANIZATIONS FOR INTERNATIONAL VOLUNTEER
SERVICE (FOCSIV), PAUL VI AUDIENCE HALL
THURSDAY, DECEMBER 4, 2014

Pope Francis @Pontifex · June 18, 2015

There is an intimate relationship between the poor and the fragility of the planet. #LaudatoSi

THE EARTH IS OUR COMMON HOME

An authentic faith—which is never comfortable or completely personal—always involves a deep desire to change the world, to transmit values, to leave this earth somehow better than we found it. We love this magnificent planet on which God has put us, and we love the human family which dwells here, with all its tragedies and struggles, its hopes and aspirations, its strengths and weaknesses. The earth is our common home and all of us are brothers and sisters.

APOSTOLIC EXHORTATION, *EVANGELII GAUDIUM*, 183
SUNDAY, NOVEMBER 24, 2013

Pope Francis @Pontifex · June 18, 2015
Earth is essentially a shared inheritance, whose fruits are meant to benefit everyone. #LaudatoSi

WE HAVE RECEIVED THIS EARTH AS AN INHERITANCE

It is urgent today for you, for me, for everyone, to keep reflecting on and talking about our current situation. And I am saying urgent that we be motivated to think about the culture, the kind of culture we want not only for ourselves, but for our children and our grandchildren. We have received this earth as an inheritance, as a gift, in trust. We would do well to ask ourselves: "What kind of world do we want to leave behind? What meaning or direction do we want to give to our lives? Why have we been put here? What is the purpose of our work and all our efforts?" (cf. *Laudato Si'*, 160). Why are we studying?

Personal initiatives are always necessary and good. But we are asked to go one step further: to start viewing reality in an organic and not fragmented way, to ask about where we stand in relation to others, inasmuch as "everything is interconnected" (*Laudato Si'*, 138). There is no right to exclusion.

ADDRESS TO EDUCATORS, PONTIFICAL CATHOLIC
UNIVERSITY OF ECUADOR, QUITO
TUESDAY, JULY 7, 2015

AN ATTAINABLE IDEAL

What is involved in the creation of "a better world"? The expression does not allude naively to abstract notions or unattainable ideals; rather, it aims at an authentic and integral development, at efforts to provide dignified living conditions for everyone, at finding just responses to the needs of individuals and families, and at ensuring that God's gift of creation is respected, safeguarded and cultivated.

MESSAGE FOR THE WORLD DAY OF MIGRANTS AND
REFUGEES 2014, FROM THE VATICAN
MONDAY, AUGUST 5, 2013

Pope Francis @Pontifex · June 18, 2015

Never has humanity had such power over itself, yet nothing ensures that it will be used wisely.

OUR ULTIMATE DESTINY

The ultimate destiny of the universe is in the fullness of God, which has already been attained by the risen Christ, the measure of the maturity of all things. Here we can add yet another argument for rejecting every tyrannical and irresponsible domination of human beings over other creatures. The ultimate purpose of other creatures is not to be found in us. Rather, all creatures are moving forward with us and through us towards a common point of arrival, which is God, in that transcendent fullness where the risen Christ embraces and illumines all things. Human beings, endowed with intelligence and love, and drawn by the fullness of Christ, are called to lead all creatures back to their Creator.

ENCYCLICAL LETTER, *LAUDATO SI'*, 83
SUNDAY, MAY 24, 2015

CHAPTER THREE

~ The Roots and Consequences
of the Current Crisis ~

OUR COMMON HOME IS AT RISK

Time, my brothers and sisters, seems to be running out; we are not yet tearing one another apart, but we are tearing apart our common home. Today, the scientific community realizes what the poor have long told us: harm, perhaps irreversible harm, is being done to the ecosystem. The earth, entire peoples, and individual persons are being brutally punished. And behind all this pain, death and destruction there is the stench of what Basil of Caesarea— one of the first theologians of the Church—called "the dung of the devil." An unfettered pursuit of money rules. This is the "dung of the devil." The service of the common good is left behind. Once capital becomes an idol and guides people's decisions, once greed for money presides over the entire socioeconomic system, it ruins society, it condemns and enslaves men and women, it destroys human fraternity, it sets people against one another and, as we clearly see, it even puts at risk our common home, Sister and Mother Earth.

ADDRESS, WORLD MEETING OF POPULAR MOVEMENTS,
SANTA CRUZ DE LA SIERRA (BOLIVIA)
THURSDAY, JULY 9, 2015

THE EARTH IS BECOMING A PILE OF FILTH

Each year hundreds of millions of tons of waste are generated, much of it non-biodegradable, highly toxic and radioactive, from homes and businesses, from construction and demolition sites, from clinical, electronic and industrial sources. The earth, our home, is beginning to look more and more like an immense pile of filth. In many parts of the planet, the elderly lament that once beautiful landscapes are now covered with rubbish. Industrial waste and chemical products utilized in cities and agricultural areas can lead to bioaccumulation in the organisms of the local population, even when levels of toxins in those places are low. Frequently no measures are taken until after people's health has been irreversibly affected.

These problems are closely linked to a throwaway culture which affects the excluded just as it quickly reduces things to rubbish.

ENCYCLICAL LETTER, *LAUDATO SI'*, 21,22
SUNDAY, MAY 24, 2015

Pope Francis @Pontifex · June 18, 2015

We need only to take a frank look at the facts to see that our common home is falling into serious disrepair. #LaudatoSi

A WASTEFUL INDUSTRIAL SYSTEM

It is hard for us to accept that the way natural ecosystems work is exemplary: plants synthesize nutrients which feed herbivores; these in turn become food for carnivores, which produce significant quantities of organic waste which give rise to new generations of plants. But our industrial system, at the end of its cycle of production and consumption, has not developed the capacity to absorb and reuse waste and by-products. We have not yet managed to adopt a circular model of production capable of preserving resources for present and future generations, while limiting as much as possible the use of nonrenewable resources, moderating their consumption, maximizing their efficient use, reusing and recycling them. A serious consideration of this issue would be one way of counteracting the throwaway culture which affects the entire planet, but it must be said that only limited progress has been made in this regard.

ENCYCLICAL LETTER, *LAUDATO SI'*, 22
SUNDAY, MAY 24, 2015

Pope Francis @Pontifex · June 18, 2015

It is possible that we don't grasp the gravity of the challenges before us. #LaudatoSi

THE EARTH GROANS IN TRAVAIL

We have come to see ourselves as [Mother Earth's] lords and masters, entitled to plunder her at will. The violence present in our hearts, wounded by sin, is also reflected in the symptoms of sickness evident in the soil, in the water, in the air and in all forms of life. This is why the earth herself, burdened and laid waste, is among the most abandoned and maltreated of our poor; she "groans in travail" (Romans 8:22). We have forgotten that we ourselves are dust of the earth (cf. Genesis 2:7); our very bodies are made up of her elements, we breathe her air and we receive life and refreshment from her waters.

ENCYCLICAL LETTER, *LAUDATO SI'*, 1–2
SUNDAY, MAY 24, 2015

Pope Francis @Pontifex · June 18, 2015

We are learning all too slowly the lessons of environmental deterioration. #LaudatoSi

A DANGEROUS DETERIORATION

When the Chinese want to write the word *crisis*, they write it with two characters: the character for danger and the character for opportunity. When we speak of crises, we are speaking of dangers, but also of opportunities. This is the sense in which I am using the word. Of course every age of history contains critical elements, but in the last four centuries, we have never seen the fundamental certainties that make up human life so shaken as in our time. I am thinking of the deterioration of the environment.

MEETING WITH THE ACADEMIC AND CULTURAL WORLD, LECTURE HALL OF THE PONTIFICAL THEOLOGICAL FACULTY OF SARDINIA, CAGLIARI SUNDAY, SEPTEMBER 22, 2013

Pope Francis @Pontifex · February 15, 2016

Among the poor being treated worst is our planet. We cannot pretend all is fine in the face of the great environmental crisis.

UNHEALTHY HUMAN ENVIRONMENTS

Human beings too are creatures of this world, enjoying a right to life and happiness, and endowed with unique dignity. So we cannot fail to consider the effects on people's lives of environmental deterioration, current models of development and the throwaway culture.

Nowadays, for example, we are conscious of the disproportionate and unruly growth of many cities, which have become unhealthy to live in, not only because of pollution caused by toxic emissions but also as a result of urban chaos, poor transportation, and visual pollution and noise. Many cities are huge, inefficient structures, excessively wasteful of energy and water. Neighborhoods, even those recently built, are congested, chaotic and lacking in sufficient green space. We were not meant to be inundated by cement, asphalt, glass and metal, and deprived of physical contact with nature.

ENCYCLICAL LETTER, *LAUDATO SI'*, 43–44
SUNDAY, MAY 24, 2015

Pope Francis @Pontifex · January 19, 2016
The Gospel calls us to be close to the poor and forgotten, and to give them real hope.

A DEIFIED MARKET DEVOURS EVERYTHING

The thirst for power and possessions knows no limits. In this system, which tends to devour everything which stands in the way of increased profits, whatever is fragile, like the environment, is defenseless before the interests of a deified market, which become the only rule.

APOSTOLIC EXHORTATION, *EVANGELII GAUDIUM*, 56
SUNDAY, NOVEMBER 24, 2013

Pope Francis @Pontifex · June 18, 2015
The earth, our home, is beginning to look more and more like an immense pile of filth.

THE IDOLS OF MONEY AND PROFIT

It is no longer man who commands, but money, money, cash commands. And God our Father gave us the task of protecting the earth—not for money, but for ourselves: for men and women. We have this task! Nevertheless, men and women are sacrificed to the idols of profit and consumption: it is the "culture of waste." If a computer breaks it is a tragedy, but poverty, the needs and dramas of so many people, end up being considered normal. If on a winter's night—here on the Via Ottaviano, for example— someone dies, that is not news. If there are children in so many parts of the world who have nothing to eat, that is not news; it seems normal. It cannot be so! And yet these things enter into normality: that some homeless people should freeze to death on the street—this doesn't make news. On the contrary, when the stock market drops ten points in some cities, it constitutes a tragedy. Someone who dies is not news, but lowering income by ten points is a tragedy! In this way people are thrown aside as if they were trash.

GENERAL AUDIENCE, ST. PETER'S SQUARE
WEDNESDAY, JUNE 5, 2013

THE MENTALITY OF PROFIT AT ANY PRICE

In your letters and in our meetings, you have mentioned the many forms of exclusion and injustice which you experience in the workplace, in neighborhoods and throughout the land. They are many and diverse, just as many and diverse are the ways in which you confront them. Yet there is an invisible thread joining every one of the forms of exclusion. These are not isolated issues. Can we recognize that invisible thread which links them? I wonder whether we can see that those destructive realities are part of a system which has become global. Do we realize that that system has imposed the mentality of profit at any price, with no concern for social exclusion or the destruction of nature?

If such is the case, I would insist, let us not be afraid to say it: we want change, real change, structural change. This system is by now intolerable: farmworkers find it intolerable, laborers find it intolerable, communities find it intolerable, peoples find it intolerable.... The earth itself—our Sister, Mother Earth, as St. Francis would say—also finds it intolerable.

ADDRESS, WORLD MEETING OF POPULAR MOVEMENTS,
SANTA CRUZ DE LA SIERRA (BOLIVIA)
THURSDAY, JULY 9, 2015

Pope Francis @Pontifex · June 18, 2015
Economic interests easily end up trumping the common good.

SAY 'NO' TO AN ECONOMY OF EXCLUSION

Just as the commandment "Thou shalt not kill" sets a clear limit in order to safeguard the value of human life, today we also have to say "thou shalt not" to an economy of exclusion and inequality. Such an economy kills. How can it be that it is not a news item when an elderly homeless person dies of exposure, but it is news when the stock market loses two points? This is a case of exclusion. Can we continue to stand by when food is thrown away while people are starving? This is a case of inequality. Today everything comes under the laws of competition and the survival of the fittest, where the powerful feed upon the powerless. As a consequence, masses of people find themselves excluded and marginalized: without work, without possibilities, without any means of escape.

APOSTOLIC EXHORTATION, *EVANGELII GAUDIUM*, 53
SUNDAY, NOVEMBER 24, 2013

Pope Francis @Pontifex · June 18, 2015
There is no room for the globalization of indifference. #LaudatoSi

NO ONE IS BORN WITH GREATER RIGHTS THAN ANOTHER

We should be particularly indignant at the enormous inequalities in our midst, whereby we continue to tolerate some considering themselves more worthy than others. We fail to see that some are mired in desperate and degrading poverty, with no way out, while others have not the faintest idea of what to do with their possessions, vainly showing off their supposed superiority and leaving behind them so much waste which, if it were the case everywhere, would destroy the planet. In practice, we continue to tolerate that some consider themselves more human than others, as if they had been born with greater rights.

ENCYCLICAL LETTER, *LAUDATO SI'*, 90
SUNDAY, MAY 24, 2015

Pope Francis @Pontifex · June 18, 2015

The emptier a person's heart is, the more he or she needs to buy, own and consume. #LaudatoSi

THE CRY OF NATURE

Neglecting to monitor the harm done to nature and the environmental impact of our decisions is only the most striking sign of a disregard for the message contained in the structures of nature itself. When we fail to acknowledge as part of reality the worth of a poor person, a human embryo, a person with disabilities—to offer just a few examples—it becomes difficult to hear the cry of nature itself; everything is connected. Once the human being declares independence from reality and behaves with absolute dominion, the very foundations of our life begin to crumble, for "instead of carrying out his role as a cooperator with God in the work of creation, man sets himself up in place of God and thus ends up provoking a rebellion on the part of nature" (*Centesimus Annus*, 1991).

This situation has led to a constant schizophrenia, wherein a technocracy which sees no intrinsic value in lesser beings coexists with the other extreme, which sees no special value in human beings. But one cannot prescind from humanity. There can be no renewal of our relationship with nature without a renewal of humanity itself. There can be no ecology without an adequate anthropology.

ENCYCLICAL LETTER, *LAUDATO SI'*, 117–118
SUNDAY, MAY 24, 2015

THE CHALLENGE OF CLIMATE CHANGE

A very solid scientific consensus indicates that we are presently witnessing a disturbing warming of the climatic system. In recent decades this warming has been accompanied by a constant rise in the sea level and, it would appear, by an increase of extreme weather events, even if a scientifically determinable cause cannot be assigned to each particular phenomenon. Humanity is called to recognize the need for changes of lifestyle, production and consumption in order to combat this warming or at least the human causes which produce or aggravate it.

ENCYCLICAL LETTER, *LAUDATO SI'*, 23
SUNDAY, MAY 24, 2015

Pope Francis @Pontifex · June 18, 2015

Climate change represents one of the principal challenges facing humanity in our day. #LaudatoSi

HOUSING IS A FUNDAMENTAL RIGHT

We live nowadays in immense cities that show off proudly, even arrogantly, how modern they are. But while they offer well-being and innumerable pleasures for a happy minority, housing is denied to thousands of our neighbors...who are called elegant names such as "street people" or "people without fixed abode" or "urban campers." Isn't it curious how euphemisms abound in the world of injustices! A person, a segregated person, a person set apart, a person who suffers misery or hunger: such a one is an "urban camper." It is an elegant expression, isn't it? You should be on the lookout; I might be wrong in some cases, but in general, what lurks behind each euphemism is a crime.

We live in cities that throw up skyscrapers and shopping centers and strike big real estate deals...but they abandon a part of themselves to marginal settlements on the periphery. How painful it is to hear that poor settlements are marginalized, or, worse still, earmarked for demolition! How cruel are the images of violent evictions, bulldozers knocking down the tiny dwellings, images just like from a war. And this is what we see today.

ADDRESS TO PARTICIPANTS IN THE WORLD MEETING OF
POPULAR MOVEMENTS, OLD SYNOD HALL
TUESDAY, OCTOBER 28, 2014

WHEN THE PACE OF PRODUCTION DAMAGES MOTHER EARTH

The available resources in our world, the fruit of the intergenerational labors of peoples, and the gifts of creation more than suffice for the integral development of "each man and the whole man" (*Populorum Progressio*, 1967). The problem is of another kind. There exists a system with different aims. A system which, in addition to irresponsibly accelerating the pace of production, and using industrial and agricultural methods which damage Mother Earth in the name of "productivity," continues to deny many millions of our brothers and sisters their most elementary economic, social and cultural rights. This system runs counter to the plan of Jesus, against the Good News that Jesus brought.

ADDRESS, WORLD MEETING OF POPULAR MOVEMENTS,
SANTA CRUZ DE LA SIERRA (BOLIVIA)
THURSDAY, JULY 9, 2015

A CONFRONTATIONAL RELATIONSHIP

Men and women have constantly intervened in nature, but for a long time, this meant being in tune with and respecting the possibilities offered by the things themselves. It was a matter of receiving what nature itself allowed, as if from its own hand. Now, by contrast, we are the ones to lay our hands on things, attempting to extract everything possible from them while frequently ignoring or forgetting the reality in front of us. Human beings and material objects no longer extend a friendly hand to one another; the relationship has become confrontational. This has made it easy to accept the idea of infinite or unlimited growth, which proves so attractive to economists, financiers and experts in technology. It is based on the lie that there is an infinite supply of the earth's goods, and this leads to the planet being squeezed dry beyond every limit.

ENCYCLICAL LETTER, *LAUDATO SI'*, 106
SUNDAY, MAY 24, 2015

Pope Francis @Pontifex · October 25, 2013
The "throwaway" culture produces many bitter fruits, from wasting food to isolating many elderly people.

AN INDUSTRY OF DESTRUCTION

How greatly we need the Lord's strength to seal us with his love and his power to stop this mad race of destruction! Destroying what he has given us, the most beautiful things that he has done for us, so that we may carry them forward, nurture them to bear fruit. When I looked at the pictures in the sacristy from 71 years ago [of the bombing of the Verano on 19 July 1943], I thought, "This was so grave, so painful. That is nothing in comparison to what is happening today." Man takes control of everything, he believes he is God, he believes he is king. And wars, the wars that continue, they do not exactly help to sow the seed of life but to destroy. It is an industry of destruction. It is also a system, also of life, that when things cannot be fixed they are discarded: we discard children, we discard the old, we discard unemployed youth. This devastation has created the culture of waste. We discard people.... This is the first image that came to my mind as I listened to this reading.

HOMILY, CEMETERY OF VERANO
SOLEMNITY OF ALL SAINTS,
SATURDAY, NOVEMBER 1, 2014

ON GENETICALLY MODIFIED CROPS

Although no conclusive proof exists that GM [genetically modified] cereals may be harmful to human beings, and in some regions their use has brought about economic growth which has helped to resolve problems, there remain a number of significant difficulties which should not be underestimated. In many places, following the introduction of these crops, productive land is concentrated in the hands of a few owners due to "the progressive disappearance of small producers, who, as a consequence of the loss of the exploited lands, are obliged to withdraw from direct production" (*Una tierra para todos*, 2005). The most vulnerable of these become temporary laborers, and many rural workers end up moving to poverty-stricken urban areas. The expansion of these crops has the effect of destroying the complex network of ecosystems, diminishing the diversity of production and affecting regional economies, now and in the future.

ENCYCLICAL LETTER, *LAUDATO SI'*, 134
SUNDAY, MAY 24, 2015

CRIMES AGAINST CREATION

Let us look around: how many wounds are inflicted upon humanity by evil! Wars, violence, economic conflicts that hit the weakest, greed for money that you can't take with you and have to leave. When we were small, our grandmother used to say: "A shroud has no pocket." Love of power, corruption, divisions, crimes against human life and against creation! And—as each one of us knows and is aware—our personal sins: our failures in love and respect towards God, towards our neighbor, and towards the whole of creation.

HOMILY, ST. PETER'S SQUARE
PALM SUNDAY, MARCH 24, 2013

Pope Francis @Pontifex · June 18, 2015
Each age tends to have only a meager awareness of its own limitations.

NO PROGRESS AT THE COST OF FUTURE RESOURCES

A technological and economic development which does not leave in its wake a better world and an integrally higher quality of life cannot be considered progress. Frequently, in fact, people's quality of life actually diminishes—by the deterioration of the environment, the low quality of food or the depletion of resources—in the midst of economic growth. In this context, talk of sustainable growth usually becomes a way of distracting attention and offering excuses. It absorbs the language and values of ecology into the categories of finance and technocracy, and the social and environmental responsibility of businesses often gets reduced to a series of marketing and image-enhancing measures.

The principle of the maximization of profits, frequently isolated from other considerations, reflects a misunderstanding of the very concept of the economy. As long as production is increased, little concern is given to whether it is at the cost of future resources or the health of the environment; as long as the clearing of a forest increases production, no one calculates the losses entailed in the desertification of the land, the harm done to biodiversity or the increased pollution. In a word, businesses profit by calculating and paying only a fraction of the costs involved.

ENCYCLICAL LETTER, *LAUDATO SI'*, 194–195
SUNDAY, MAY 24, 2015

Pope Francis @Pontifex · June 18, 2015

The alliance between economy and technology ends up sidelining anything unrelated to its immediate interests.

WAR IS MADNESS

After experiencing the beauty of travelling throughout this region, where men and women work and raise their families, where children play and the elderly dream.... I now find myself here, in this place, near this cemetery, able to say only one thing: War is madness.

Whereas God carries forward the work of creation, and we men and women are called to participate in his work, war destroys. It also ruins the most beautiful work of his hands: human beings. War ruins everything, even the bonds between brothers. War is irrational; its only plan is to bring destruction: it seeks to grow by destroying....

With the heart of a son, a brother, a father, I ask each of you, indeed for all of us, to have a conversion of heart: to move on from "What does it matter to me?" to tears: for each one of the fallen of this "senseless massacre," for all the victims of the mindless wars, in every age. Weeping. Brothers and sisters, humanity needs to weep, and this is the time to weep.

HOMILY, MILITARY MEMORIAL OF REDIPUGLIA
(100TH ANNIVERSARY OF THE OUTBREAK OF FIRST
WORLD WAR)
SATURDAY, SEPTEMBER 13, 2014

RURAL COMMUNITIES AT RISK

Nowadays, it is sad to see that land, housing and work are ever more distant for the majority. It is strange but, if I talk about this, some say that the pope is communist. They do not understand that love for the poor is at the center of the Gospel. Land, housing and work, what you struggle for, are sacred rights. To make this claim is nothing unusual; it is the social teaching of the Church....

At the beginning of creation, God created man and woman, stewards of his work, mandating them to till and to keep it (cf. Genesis 2:15). I notice dozens of farmworkers (*campesinos*) here, and I want to congratulate you for caring for the land, for cultivating it and for doing so in community. The elimination of so many brothers and sisters *campesinos* worries me, and it is not because of wars or natural disasters that they are uprooted. Land and water grabbing, deforestation, and unsuitable pesticides are some of the evils which uproot people from their native land. This wretched separation is not only physical but existential and spiritual as well, because there is a relationship with the land, such that rural communities and their special way of life are being put at flagrant risk of decline and even of extinction.

ADDRESS TO PARTICIPANTS IN THE WORLD MEETING OF POPULAR MOVEMENTS, OLD SYNOD HALL TUESDAY, OCTOBER 28, 2014

Pope Francis @Pontifex · September 4, 2015

War is the mother of all poverty, a vast predator of lives and souls.

HUMAN BEINGS AS CONSUMER GOODS

There is no worse material poverty than the poverty which does not allow people to earn their bread, which deprives them of the dignity of work. But youth unemployment, informality or underground work, and the lack of labor rights are not inevitable. These are the result of an underlying social choice in favor of an economic system that puts profit above man. If economic profit takes precedence over the individual and over humanity, we find a throwaway culture at work that considers humanity in itself, human beings, as a consumer good, which can be used and then thrown away.

This happens when the deity of money is at the center of an economic system rather than man, the human person. Yes, at the center of every social or economic system must be the person, image of God, created to "have dominion over" the universe. The inversion of values happens when the person is displaced and money becomes the deity.

ADDRESS TO PARTICIPANTS IN THE WORLD MEETING OF
POPULAR MOVEMENTS, OLD SYNOD HALL
TUESDAY, OCTOBER 28, 2014

YOU ARE YOUR BROTHER'S KEEPER!

When man thinks only of himself, of his own interests and places himself in the center…then all relationships are broken and everything is ruined; then the door opens to violence, indifference, and conflict. This is precisely what the passage in the book of Genesis seeks to teach us in the story of the Fall: man enters into conflict with himself, he realizes that he is naked and he hides himself because he is afraid, he is afraid of God's glance; he accuses the woman, she who is flesh of his flesh…he breaks harmony with creation, he begins to raise his hand against his brother to kill him. Can we say that from harmony he passes to "disharmony"? No, there is no such thing as "disharmony"; there is either harmony or we fall into chaos, where there is violence, argument, conflict, fear.…

It is exactly in this chaos that God asks man's conscience: "Where is Abel your brother?" and Cain responds: "I do not know; am I my brother's keeper?" (Genesis 4:9). We too are asked this question, it would be good for us to ask ourselves as well: Am I really my brother's keeper? Yes, you are your brother's keeper! To be human means to care for one another!

VIGIL, PRAYER FOR PEACE, ST. PETER'S SQUARE
SATURDAY, SEPTEMBER 7, 2013

ACCESS TO DRINKING WATER

One very serious problem...is the lack of access to infrastructures and basic services. By this I mean toilets, sewers, drains, refuse collection, electricity, roads, as well as schools, hospitals, recreational and sport centers, studios and workshops for artists and craftsmen. I refer in particular to access to drinking water.... To deny a family water, under any bureaucratic pretext whatsoever, is a great injustice, especially when one profits from this need.

ADDRESS, KANGEMI SLUM, NAIROBI (KENYA)
FRIDAY, NOVEMBER 27, 2015

Pope Francis @Pontifex · June 18, 2015

One particularly serious problem is the quality of water available to the poor. #LaudatoSi

A NEW MODEL OF DEVELOPMENT

Kenya is a country that characterizes the global challenge of our time: to protect creation by reshaping the model of development to be equitable, inclusive and sustainable. All this can be seen in Nairobi, the largest city in East Africa, where wealth and poverty coexist: this is a scandal! Not only in Africa but here too, everywhere. The coexistence of wealth and poverty is a scandal, it is a disgrace for humanity. Nairobi is where the Office of the United Nations Environmental Program, which I visited, is located. In Kenya I met the authorities and diplomats, and also the residents of a poor neighborhood; I met the leaders of various Christian confessions and of other religions, priests and consecrated people. I met young people, so many young people! On each occasion I encouraged them to treasure the great wealth of that country: the natural and spiritual wealth, made up of the earth's resources, of the younger generations and of the values that shape the wisdom of the people. In today's tragic context I had the joy of bringing Jesus's word of hope: "Stand strong in faith, do not be afraid."

GENERAL AUDIENCE, ST. PETER'S SQUARE
WEDNESDAY, DECEMBER 2, 2015

WE NEED CHANGE

The Bible tells us that God hears the cry of his people, and I wish to join my voice to yours in calling for the three L's for all our brothers and sisters: land, lodging and labor. I said it and I repeat it: these are sacred rights. It is important, it is well worth fighting for them. May the cry of the excluded be heard in Latin America and throughout the world.

Before all else, let us begin by acknowledging that change is needed. Here I would clarify, lest there be any misunderstanding, that I am speaking about problems common to all Latin Americans and, more generally, to humanity as a whole. They are global problems which today no one state can resolve on its own. With this clarification, I now propose that we ask the following questions:

Do we realize that something is wrong in a world where there are so many farmworkers without land, so many families without a home, so many laborers without rights, so many persons whose dignity is not respected?

Do we realize that something is wrong where so many senseless wars are being fought and acts of fratricidal violence are taking place on our very doorstep? Do we realize something is wrong when the soil, water, air and living creatures of our world are under constant threat?

So, if we do realize all this, let's not be afraid to say it: we need change; we want change.

ADDRESS, WORLD MEETING OF POPULAR MOVEMENTS,
SANTA CRUZ DE LA SIERRA (BOLIVIA)
THURSDAY, JULY 9, 2015

Pope Francis @Pontifex · June 18, 2015
I invite all to pause to think about the challenges we face regarding care for our common home. #LaudatoSi

CHAPTER FOUR

~ Called to Protect God's Handiwork ~

RETURN TO SIMPLICITY

Christian spirituality proposes an alternative understanding of the quality of life and encourages a prophetic and contemplative lifestyle, one capable of deep enjoyment free of the obsession with consumption. We need to take up an ancient lesson found in different religious traditions and also in the Bible. It is the conviction that "less is more." A constant flood of new consumer goods can baffle the heart and prevent us from cherishing each thing and each moment. To be serenely present to each reality, however small it may be, opens us to much greater horizons of understanding and personal fulfillment. Christian spirituality proposes a growth marked by moderation and the capacity to be happy with little. It is a return to that simplicity which allows us to stop and appreciate the small things, to be grateful for the opportunities which life affords us, to be spiritually detached from what we possess, and not to succumb to sadness for what we lack.

ENCYCLICAL LETTER, *LAUDATO SI'*, 222
SUNDAY, MAY 24, 2015

ABANDON A SELFISH LIFESTYLE

When a person discovers God, the true treasure, he abandons a selfish lifestyle and seeks to share with others the charity which comes from God. He who becomes a friend of God loves his brothers and sisters, commits himself to safeguarding their life and their health, and also to respecting the environment and nature.

HOMILY, PARK OF THE ROYAL PALACE OF CASERTA
SATURDAY, JULY 26, 2014

Pope Francis @Pontifex · April 24, 2014

A simple lifestyle is good for us, helping us to better share with those in need.

PRACTICE THE WAY OF LOVE

St. Thérèseof Lisieux invites us to practice the little way of love, not to miss out on a kind word, a smile or any small gesture which sows peace and friendship. An integral ecology is also made up of simple daily gestures which break with the logic of violence, exploitation and selfishness. In the end, a world of exacerbated consumption is at the same time a world which mistreats life in all its forms.

ENCYCLICAL LETTER, *LAUDATO SI'*, 230
SUNDAY, MAY 24, 2015

Pope Francis @Pontifex · March 12, 2015

Beware of getting too comfortable! When we are comfortable, it's easy to forget other people.

PROTECT THIS FRAGILE WORLD

Small yet strong in the love of God, like St. Francis of Assisi, all of us, as Christians, are called to watch over and protect the fragile world in which we live, and all its peoples.

APOSTOLIC EXHORTATION, *EVANGELII GAUDIUM*, 216
SUNDAY, NOVEMBER 24, 2013

Pope Francis @Pontifex · July 10, 2013

If we wish to follow Christ closely, we cannot choose an easy, quiet life. It will be a demanding life, but full of joy.

THE DESIRE TO CHANGE

A healthy relationship with creation is one dimension of overall personal conversion, which entails the recognition of our errors, sins, faults and failures, and leads to heartfelt repentance and desire to change. The Australian bishops spoke of the importance of such conversion for achieving reconciliation with creation: "To achieve such reconciliation, we must examine our lives and acknowledge the ways in which we have harmed God's creation through our actions and our failure to act. We need to experience a conversion, or change of heart."

ENCYCLICAL LETTER, *LAUDATO SI'*, 218
SUNDAY, MAY 24, 2015

INSTRUMENTS OF GOD

Never have we so hurt and mistreated our common home as we have in the last two hundred years. Yet we are called to be instruments of God our Father so that our planet might be what he desired when he created it and correspond with his plan for peace, beauty and fullness.

ENCYCLICAL LETTER, *LAUDATO SI'*, 53
SUNDAY, MAY 24, 2015

Pope Francis @Pontifex · Sep 5, 2013

There is no such thing as low-cost Christianity. Following Jesus means swimming against the tide, renouncing evil and selfishness.

VIRTUOUS HABITS

Some committed and prayerful Christians, with the excuse of realism and pragmatism, tend to ridicule expressions of concern for the environment. Others are passive; they choose not to change their habits and thus become inconsistent. So what they all need is an "ecological conversion," whereby the effects of their encounter with Jesus Christ become evident in their relationship with the world around them. Living our vocation to be protectors of God's handiwork is essential to a life of virtue; it is not an optional or a secondary aspect of our Christian experience.

ENCYCLICAL LETTER, *LAUDATO SI'*, 217
SUNDAY, MAY 24, 2015

THE PROBLEM OF WASTE

There was a time when our grandparents were very careful not to throw away any leftover food. Consumerism has induced us to be accustomed to excess and to the daily waste of food, whose value, which goes far beyond mere financial parameters, we are no longer able to judge correctly.

Let us remember well, however, that whenever food is thrown out it is as if it were stolen from the table of the poor, from the hungry! I ask everyone to reflect on the problem of the loss and waste of food, to identify ways and approaches which, by seriously dealing with this problem, convey solidarity and sharing with the underprivileged.

GENERAL AUDIENCE, ST. PETER'S SQUARE
WEDNESDAY, JUNE 5, 2013

Pope Francis @Pontifex · June 18, 2015
We know how unsustainable is the behavior of those who constantly consume and destroy.

DAILY ACTIONS MAKE A DIFFERENCE

Only by cultivating sound virtues will people be able to make a selfless ecological commitment. A person who could afford to spend and consume more but regularly uses less heating and wears warmer clothes shows the kind of convictions and attitudes which help to protect the environment. There is a nobility in the duty to care for creation through little daily actions, and it is wonderful how education can bring about real changes in lifestyle. Education in environmental responsibility can encourage ways of acting which directly and significantly affect the world around us, such as avoiding the use of plastic and paper, reducing water consumption, separating refuse, cooking only what can reasonably be consumed, showing care for other living beings, using public transport or carpooling, planting trees, turning off unnecessary lights, or any number of other practices. All of these reflect a generous and worthy creativity which brings out the best in human beings. Reusing something instead of immediately discarding it, when done for the right reasons, can be an act of love which expresses our own dignity.

ENCYCLICAL LETTER, *LAUDATO SI'*, 211
SUNDAY, MAY 24, 2015

DON'T LOSE HEART!

What can I do, as collector of paper, old clothes or used metal, a recycler, about all these problems if I barely make enough money to put food on the table? What can I do as a craftsman, a street vendor, a trucker, a downtrodden worker, if I don't even enjoy workers' rights? What can I do, a farmwife, a native woman, a fisher who can hardly fight the domination of the big corporations? What can I do from my little home, my shanty, my hamlet, my settlement, when I daily meet with discrimination and marginalization? What can be done by those students, those young people, those activists, those missionaries who come to a neighborhood with their hearts full of hopes and dreams, but without any real solution for their problems? They can do a lot. They really can. You, the lowly, the exploited, the poor and underprivileged, can do, and are doing, a lot. I would even say that the future of humanity is in great measure in your own hands, through your ability to organize and carry out creative alternatives,

through your daily efforts to ensure the three "L's"—
do you agree?—(labor, lodging, land) and through your
proactive participation in the great processes of change on
the national, regional and global levels. Don't lose heart!

ADDRESS, WORLD MEETING OF POPULAR MOVEMENTS,
SANTA CRUZ DE LA SIERRA (BOLIVIA)
THURSDAY, JULY 9, 2015

Pope Francis @Pontifex · August 23, 2013
Lord, teach us to step outside ourselves. Teach us to go out
into the streets and manifest your love.

YOU HAVE AN IMPORTANT CONTRIBUTION TO MAKE

You are called to care for creation not only as responsible citizens, but also as followers of Christ! Respect for the environment means more than simply using cleaner products or recycling what we use. These are important aspects, but not enough. We need to see, with the eyes of faith, the beauty of God's saving plan, the link between the natural environment and the dignity of the human person. Men and women are made in the image and likeness of God and given dominion over creation (cf. Genesis 1:26–28). As stewards of God's creation, we are called to make the earth a beautiful garden for the human family. When we destroy our forests, ravage our soil and pollute our seas, we betray that noble calling....

Dear young people, the just use and stewardship of the earth's resources is an urgent task, and you have an important contribution to make.

ADDRESS TO YOUNG PEOPLE, SPORTS FIELD OF SANTO TOMAS UNIVERSITY, MANILA (PHILIPPINES) SUNDAY, JANUARY 18, 2015

THE FUTURE IS UP TO US

What kind of world do we want to leave to those who come after us, to children who are now growing up? This question not only concerns the environment in isolation; the issue cannot be approached piecemeal. When we ask ourselves what kind of world we want to leave behind, we think in the first place of its general direction, its meaning and its values. Unless we struggle with these deeper issues, I do not believe that our concern for ecology will produce significant results. But if these issues are courageously faced, we are led inexorably to ask other pointed questions: What is the purpose of our life in this world? Why are we here? What is the goal of our work and all our efforts? What need does the earth have of us? It is no longer enough, then, simply to state that we should be concerned for future generations. We need to see that what is at stake is our own dignity. Leaving an inhabitable planet to future generations is, first and foremost, up to us. The issue is one which dramatically affects us, for it has to do with the ultimate meaning of our earthly sojourn.

ENCYCLICAL LETTER, *LAUDATO SI'*, 160
SUNDAY, MAY 24, 2015

THE PATH OF RENEWAL

Many things have to change course, but it is we human beings above all who need to change. We lack an awareness of our common origin, of our mutual belonging, and of a future to be shared with everyone. This basic awareness would enable the development of new convictions, attitudes and forms of life. A great cultural, spiritual and educational challenge stands before us, and it will demand that we set out on the long path of renewal.

ENCYCLICAL LETTER, *LAUDATO SI'*, 202
SUNDAY, MAY 24, 2015

Pope Francis @Pontifex · June 18, 2015
Leaving an inhabitable planet to future generations is, first and foremost, up to us.

WE MUST KEEP WATCH OVER OURSELVES

I would like to ask all those who have positions of responsibility in economic, political and social life, and all men and women of goodwill: let us be "protectors" of creation, protectors of God's plan inscribed in nature, protectors of one another and of the environment. Let us not allow omens of destruction and death to accompany the advance of this world! But to be "protectors," we also have to keep watch over ourselves! Let us not forget that hatred, envy and pride defile our lives! Being protectors, then, also means keeping watch over our emotions, over our hearts, because they are the seat of good and evil intentions: intentions that build up and tear down! We must not be afraid of goodness or even tenderness!

HOMILY, ST. PETER'S SQUARE, MASS FOR THE
INAUGURATION OF THE PONTIFICATE
TUESDAY, MARCH 19, 2013

Pope Francis @Pontifex · June 19, 2015
Lord, seize us with your power and light, help us to protect all life, to prepare for a better future. #LaudatoSi

LIVE FULLY YOUR CONVERSION

God created the world, writing into it an order and a dynamism that human beings have no right to ignore. We read in the Gospel that Jesus says of the birds of the air that "not one of them is forgotten before God" (Luke 12:6). How then can we possibly mistreat them or cause them harm? I ask all Christians to recognize and to live fully this dimension of their conversion. May the power and the light of the grace we have received also be evident in our relationship to other creatures and to the world around us. In this way, we will help nurture that sublime fraternity with all creation which St. Francis of Assisi so radiantly embodied.

ENCYCLICAL LETTER, *LAUDATO SI'*, 221
SUNDAY, MAY 24, 2015

Pope Francis @Pontifex · March 27, 2013
Being with Jesus demands that we go out from ourselves, and from living a tired and habitual faith.

A NEW CONVERSATION

The urgent challenge to protect our common home includes a concern to bring the whole human family together to seek a sustainable and integral development, for we know that things can change. The Creator does not abandon us; he never forsakes his loving plan or repents of having created us. Humanity still has the ability to work together in building our common home....

I urgently appeal, then, for a new dialogue about how we are shaping the future of our planet. We need a conversation which includes everyone, since the environmental challenge we are undergoing, and its human roots, concern and affect us all.

ENCYCLICAL LETTER, *LAUDATO SI'*, 13–14
SUNDAY, MAY 24, 2015

Pope Francis @Pontifex · June 18, 2015
Many things have to change course, but it is we human beings above all who need to change.

THE POWER OF GRASSROOTS MOVEMENTS

Grassroots movements express the urgent need to revitalize our democracies, so often hijacked by innumerable factors. It is impossible to imagine a future for society without the active participation of great majorities as protagonists, and such proactive participation overflows the logical procedures of formal democracy. Moving towards a world of lasting peace and justice calls us to go beyond paternalistic forms of assistance; it calls us to create new forms of participation that include popular movements and invigorate local, national and international governing structures with that torrent of moral energy that springs from including the excluded in the building of a common destiny. And all this with a constructive spirit, without resentment, with love.

ADDRESS, WORLD MEETING OF POPULAR MOVEMENTS,
OLD SYNOD HALL
TUESDAY, OCTOBER 28, 2014

A NEW ATTITUDE OF THE HEART

Nature is filled with words of love, but how can we listen to them amid constant noise, interminable and nerve-wracking distractions, or the cult of appearances? Many people today sense a profound imbalance which drives them to frenetic activity and makes them feel busy, in a constant hurry which in turn leads them to ride roughshod over everything around them. An integral ecology includes taking time to recover a serene harmony with creation, reflecting on our lifestyle and our ideals....

We are speaking of an attitude of the heart, one which approaches life with serene attentiveness, which is capable of being fully present to someone without thinking of what comes next, which accepts each moment as a gift from God to be lived to the full. Jesus taught us this attitude when he invited us to contemplate the lilies of the field and the birds of the air, or when seeing the rich young man and knowing his restlessness, "he looked at him with love" (Mark 10:21). He was completely present to everyone and to everything, and in this way he showed us the way to overcome that unhealthy anxiety which makes us superficial, aggressive and compulsive consumers.

ENCYCLICAL LETTER, *LAUDATO SI'*, 225–226
SUNDAY, MAY 24, 2015

YOU ARE SOWERS OF CHANGE

Here in Bolivia I have heard a phrase which I like: "process of change." Change seen not as something which will one day result from any one political decision or change in social structure. We know from painful experience that changes of structure which are not accompanied by a sincere conversion of mind and heart sooner or later end up in bureaucratization, corruption and failure. There must be a change of heart. That is why I like the image of a "process," processes, where the drive to sow, to water seeds which others will see sprout, replaces the ambition to occupy every available position of power and to see immediate results. The option is to bring about processes and not to occupy positions. Each of us is just one part of a complex and differentiated whole, interacting in time: peoples who struggle to find meaning, a destiny, and to live with dignity, to "live well," and in that sense, worthily.

ADDRESS, WORLD MEETING OF POPULAR MOVEMENTS,
SANTA CRUZ DE LA SIERRA (BOLIVIA)
THURSDAY, JULY 9, 2015

DECISIVE ACTION, HERE AND NOW

Doomsday predictions can no longer be met with irony or disdain. We may well be leaving to coming generations debris, desolation and filth. The pace of consumption, waste and environmental change has so stretched the planet's capacity that our contemporary lifestyle, unsustainable as it is, can only precipitate catastrophes, such as those which even now periodically occur in different areas of the world. The effects of the present imbalance can only be reduced by our decisive action, here and now. We need to reflect on our accountability before those who will have to endure the dire consequences.

ENCYCLICAL LETTER, *LAUDATO SI'*, 161
SUNDAY, MAY 24, 2015

Pope Francis @Pontifex · November 25, 2013
To live charitably means not looking out for our own interests, but carrying the burdens of the weakest and poorest among us.

CREATING NETWORKS OF SOLIDARITY

An admirable creativity and generosity is shown by persons and groups who respond to environmental limitations by alleviating the adverse effects of their surroundings and learning to orient their lives amid disorder and uncertainty. For example, in some places, where the façades of buildings are derelict, people show great care for the interior of their homes or find contentment in the kindness and friendliness of others. A wholesome social life can light up a seemingly undesirable environment. At times a commendable human ecology is practiced by the poor despite numerous hardships. The feeling of asphyxiation brought on by densely populated residential areas is countered if close and warm relationships develop, if communities are created, if the limitations of the environment are compensated for in the interior of each person who feels held within a network of solidarity and belonging. In this way, any place can turn from being a hell on earth into the setting for a dignified life.

ENCYCLICAL LETTER, *LAUDATO SI'*, 148
SUNDAY, MAY 24, 2015

A CYCLONE OF HOPE

The scandal of poverty cannot be addressed by promoting strategies of containment that only tranquilize the poor and render them tame and inoffensive. How sad it is when we find, behind allegedly altruistic works, the other being reduced to passivity or being negated; or worse still, we find hidden personal agendas or commercial interests. "Hypocrites" is what Jesus would say to those responsible. How marvelous it is, by contrast, when we see peoples moving forward, especially their young and their poorest members. Then one feels a promising breeze that revives hope for a better world. May this breeze become a cyclone of hope. This is my wish.

ADDRESS, WORLD MEETING OF POPULAR MOVEMENTS,
OLD SYNOD HALL
TUESDAY, OCTOBER 28, 2014

Pope Francis @Pontifex · June 20, 2014
There is so much indifference in the face of suffering. May we overcome indifference with concrete acts of charity.

A REVOLUTIONARY PLAN OF ACTION

We talk about land, work, housing ... we talk about working for peace and taking care of nature. Why are we accustomed to seeing decent work destroyed, countless families evicted, rural farmworkers driven off the land, war waged and nature abused? Because in this system, man, the human person, has been removed from the center and replaced by something else. Because idolatrous worship is devoted to money. Because indifference has been globalized: "Why should I care what happens to others as long as I can defend what's mine?" Because the world has forgotten God, who is Father; and by setting God aside, it has made itself an orphan.

Some of you said that this system cannot endure. We must change it. We must put human dignity back at the center and on that pillar build the alternative social structures we need. This must be done with courage but also with intelligence, with tenacity but without fanaticism, with passion yet without violence. And all of us together, addressing the conflicts without getting trapped in them, always seeking to resolve the tensions in order to reach a higher plane of unity, of peace and of justice. We Christians have something very lovely, a guide to action, a program we could call revolutionary. I earnestly recommend that you read it: the Beatitudes in St. Matthew chapter 5 (cf. Matthew 5:3) and in St. Luke chapter 6 (cf. Luke 6:20); and the Last Judgment passage in St. Matthew chapter 25. This is what I told the young people at Rio de Janeiro: With these passages, you have the plan of action.

ADDRESS, WORLD MEETING OF POPULAR MOVEMENTS,
OLD SYNOD HALL
TUESDAY, OCTOBER 28, 2014

Pope Francis @Pontifex · April 3, 2014
May we never get used to the poverty and decay around us. A Christian must act.

GUIDED BY OUR DEEPEST CONVICTIONS

Believers themselves must constantly feel challenged to live in a way consonant with their faith and not to contradict it by their actions. They need to be encouraged to be ever open to God's grace and to draw constantly from their deepest convictions about love, justice and peace. If a mistaken understanding of our own principles has at times led us to justify mistreating nature, to exercise tyranny over creation, to engage in war, injustice and acts of violence, we believers should acknowledge that by so doing we were not faithful to the treasures of wisdom which we have been called to protect and preserve.

ENCYCLICAL LETTER, *LAUDATO SI'*, 200
SUNDAY, MAY 24, 2015

Pope Francis @Pontifex · June 18, 2015
Believers must feel challenged to live in a way consonant with their faith. #LaudatoSi

WE MUST RAISE OUR VOICES

From now on, every worker, within the formal system of salaried employment or outside it, should have the right to decent remuneration, to social security and to a pension. Among you here are waste-collectors, recyclers, peddlers, seamstresses or tailors, artisans, fishermen, farmworkers, builders, miners, workers in previously abandoned enterprises, members of all kinds of cooperatives and workers in grassroots jobs who are excluded from labor rights, who are denied the possibility of unionizing, whose income is neither adequate nor stable. Today I want to join my voice to yours and support you in your struggle.

There cannot be land, there cannot be housing, there cannot be work if we do not have peace and if we destroy the planet. These are such important topics that the peoples of the world and their popular organizations cannot fail to debate them. This cannot just remain in the hands of political leaders. All peoples of the earth, all men and women of good will—all of us must raise our voices in defense of these two precious gifts: peace and nature.

ADDRESS, WORLD MEETING OF POPULAR MOVEMENTS,
OLD SYNOD HALL
TUESDAY, OCTOBER 28, 2014

GENUINE INTERPERSONAL ENCOUNTER

Each day you are caught up in the storms of people's lives....You, dear brothers and sisters, often work on little things, in local situations, amid forms of injustice which you do not simply accept but actively resist, standing up to an idolatrous system which excludes, debases and kills. I have seen you work tirelessly for the soil and crops of *campesinos*, for their lands and communities, for a more dignified local economy, for the urbanization of their homes and settlements; you have helped them build their own homes and develop neighborhood infrastructures.

This rootedness in the barrio, the land, the office, the labor union, this ability to see yourselves in the faces of others, this daily proximity to their share of troubles— because they exist and we all have them—and their little acts of heroism: this is what enables you to practice the commandment of love, not on the basis of ideas or concepts, but rather on the basis of genuine interpersonal encounter.

ADDRESS, WORLD MEETING OF POPULAR MOVEMENTS,
SANTA CRUZ DE LA SIERRA (BOLIVIA)
THURSDAY, JULY 9, 2015

LOCAL GROUPS MAKING A REAL DIFFERENCE

In some places, cooperatives are being developed to exploit renewable sources of energy which ensure local self-sufficiency and even the sale of surplus energy. This simple example shows that, while the existing world order proves powerless to assume its responsibilities, local individuals and groups can make a real difference. They are able to instill a greater sense of responsibility, a strong sense of community, a readiness to protect others, a spirit of creativity and a deep love for the land. They are also concerned about what they will eventually leave to their children and grandchildren. These values are deeply rooted in indigenous peoples.

ENCYCLICAL LETTER, *LAUDATO SI'*, 179
SUNDAY, MAY 24, 2015

Pope Francis @Pontifex · June 18, 2015

What kind of world do we want to leave to those who come after us, to children who are now growing up?

OXYGEN FOR THE WORLD

We need to build up this culture of encounter. We do not love concepts or ideas; no one loves a concept or an idea. We love people. Commitment—true commitment—is born of the love of men and women, of children and the elderly, of peoples and communities, of names and faces which fill our hearts. From those seeds of hope patiently sown in the forgotten fringes of our planet, from those seedlings of a tenderness which struggles to grow amid the shadows of exclusion, great trees will spring up, great groves of hope to give oxygen to our world.

So I am pleased to see that you are working at close hand to care for those seedlings, but at the same time, with a broader perspective, to protect the entire forest. Your work is carried out against a horizon which, while concentrating on your own specific area, also aims to resolve at their root the more general problems of poverty, inequality and exclusion.

ADDRESS, WORLD MEETING OF POPULAR MOVEMENTS,
SANTA CRUZ DE LA SIERRA (BOLIVIA)
THURSDAY, JULY 9, 2015

WE NEED ONE ANOTHER

Care for nature is part of a lifestyle which includes the capacity for living together and communion.... We must regain the conviction that we need one another, that we have a shared responsibility for others and the world, and that being good and decent are worth it. We have had enough of immorality and the mockery of ethics, goodness, faith and honesty. It is time to acknowledge that lighthearted superficiality has done us no good. When the foundations of social life are corroded, what ensues are battles over conflicting interests, new forms of violence and brutality, and obstacles to the growth of a genuine culture of care for the environment.

ENCYCLICAL LETTER, *LAUDATO SI'*, 228–229
SUNDAY, MAY 24, 2015

Pope Francis @Pontifex · June 11, 2013
We must not be afraid of solidarity; rather let us make all we have and are available to God.

WALK AND PRAY TOGETHER

The world, looking to us believers, exhorts us to cooperate amongst ourselves and with the men and women of good will who profess no religion, asking us for effective responses regarding numerous issues: peace, hunger, the poverty that afflicts millions of people, the environmental crisis, violence, especially that committed in the name of religion, corruption, moral decay, the crisis of the family, of the economy, of finance, and especially of hope. We believers have no recipe for these problems, but we have one great resource: prayer. We believers pray. We must pray. Prayer is our treasure, from which we draw according to our respective traditions, to request the gifts that humanity longs for....

We can walk together, taking care of one another and of creation. All believers of every religion. Together we can praise the Creator for giving us the garden of the world to till and keep as a common good, and we can achieve shared plans to overcome poverty and to ensure to every man and woman the conditions for a dignified life.

INTERRELIGIOUS GENERAL AUDIENCE,
50TH ANNIVERSARY OF "NOSTRA AETATE,"
ST. PETER'S SQUARE
WEDNESDAY, OCTOBER 28, 2015

BE AGENTS OF MERCY

How many deserts, even today, do human beings need to cross! Above all, the desert within, when we have no love for God or neighbor, when we fail to realize that we are guardians of all that the Creator has given us and continues to give us. God's mercy can make even the driest land become a garden, can restore life to dry bones (cf. Ezra 37:1–14).

So this is the invitation which I address to everyone: Let us accept the grace of Christ's Resurrection! Let us be renewed by God's mercy, let us be loved by Jesus, let us enable the power of his love to transform our lives too, and let us become agents of this mercy, channels through which God can water the earth, protect all creation and make justice and peace flourish.

URBI ET ORBI MESSAGE
EASTER SUNDAY, MARCH 31, 2013

Pope Francis @Pontifex · September 17, 2013
There are many people in need in today's world. Am I self-absorbed in my own concerns or am I aware of those who need help?

I AM WITH YOU!

I would like to repeat: the future of humanity does not lie solely in the hands of great leaders, the great powers and the elites. It is fundamentally in the hands of peoples and in their ability to organize. It is in their hands, which can guide with humility and conviction this process of change. I am with you. Each of us, let me repeat from the heart: no family without lodging, no rural worker without land, no laborer without rights, no people without sovereignty, no individual without dignity, no child without childhood, no young person without a future, no elderly person without a venerable old age. Keep up your struggle and, please, take great care of Mother Earth.... I ask God our Father to accompany you and to bless you, to fill you with his love and defend you on your way by granting you in abundance that strength which keeps us on our feet: that strength is hope. It is something important: hope does not disappoint. I ask you, please, to pray for me. If some of you are unable to pray, with all respect, I ask you to send me your good thoughts and energy.

ADDRESS, WORLD MEETING OF POPULAR MOVEMENTS,
SANTA CRUZ DE LA SIERRA (BOLIVIA)

THURSDAY, JULY 9, 2015

CHAPTER FIVE

~ Towards a Healthier Planet ~

A TIME FOR COURAGE AND ACTION

In *Laudato Si'* I call for a courageous and responsible effort to "redirect our steps" and to avert the most serious effects of the environmental deterioration caused by human activity. I am convinced that we can make a difference and I have no doubt that the United States—and this Congress—have an important role to play. Now is the time for courageous actions and strategies.

ADDRESS TO THE JOINT SESSION OF THE UNITED STATES
CONGRESS, WASHINGTON, D.C.
THURSDAY, SEPTEMBER 24, 2015

Pope Francis @Pontifex · June 18, 2015
There is an urgent need for us to move forward in a bold cultural revolution. #LaudatoSi

HOPE FOR HUMANITY

In recent decades, environmental issues have given rise to considerable public debate and have elicited a variety of committed and generous civic responses. Politics and business have been slow to react in a way commensurate with the urgency of the challenges facing our world. Although the post-industrial period may well be remembered as one of the most irresponsible in history, nonetheless there is reason to hope that humanity at the dawn of the twenty-first century will be remembered for having generously shouldered its grave responsibilities.

ENCYCLICAL LETTER, *LAUDATO SI'*, 165–166
SUNDAY, MAY 24, 2015

Pope Francis @Pontifex · May 1, 2014
I ask everyone with political responsibility to remember two things: human dignity and the common good.

WE MUST DEFEND MOTHER EARTH

Our common home is being pillaged, laid waste and harmed with impunity. Cowardice in defending it is a grave sin. We see with growing disappointment how one international summit after another takes place without any significant result. There exists a clear, definite and pressing ethical imperative to implement what has not yet been done. We cannot allow certain interests—interests which are global but not universal—to take over, to dominate states and international organizations, and to continue destroying creation. People and their movements are called to cry out, to mobilize and to demand—peacefully, but firmly—that appropriate and urgently needed measures be taken. I ask you, in the name of God, to defend Mother Earth.

ADDRESS, WORLD MEETING OF POPULAR MOVEMENTS,
SANTA CRUZ DE LA SIERRA (BOLIVIA)
THURSDAY, JULY 9, 2015

THE PATRIMONY OF ALL

The natural environment is a collective good, the patrimony of all humanity and the responsibility of everyone. If we make something our own, it is only to administer it for the good of all. If we do not, we burden our consciences with the weight of having denied the existence of others. That is why the New Zealand bishops asked what the commandment "Thou shall not kill" means when "twenty percent of the world's population consumes resources at a rate that robs the poor nations and future generations of what they need to survive."

ENCYCLICAL LETTER, *LAUDATO SI'*, 95
SUNDAY, MAY 24, 2015

Pope Francis @Pontifex · April 25, 2014
We must not let ourselves fall into the vortex of pessimism. Faith can move mountains!

WE CAN NO LONGER TURN OUR BACKS

There is a relationship between our life and that of Mother Earth, between the way we live and the gift we have received from God. "The human environment and the natural environment deteriorate together; we cannot adequately combat environmental degradation unless we attend to causes related to human and social degradation" (*Laudato Si'*, 48). Yet just as both can "deteriorate," we can also say that they can "support one another and can be changed for the better." This reciprocal relationship can lead to openness, transformation, and life—or to destruction and death.

One thing is certain: we can no longer turn our backs on reality, on our brothers and sisters, on Mother Earth. It is wrong to turn aside from what is happening all around us, as if certain situations did not exist or have nothing to do with our life. It is not right for us, nor is it even humane to get caught up in the play of a throwaway culture.

ADDRESS TO EDUCATORS, PONTIFICAL CATHOLIC
UNIVERSITY OF ECUADOR, QUITO
TUESDAY, JULY 7, 2015

SEEK EFFECTIVE SOLUTIONS

In effect, a selfish and boundless thirst for power and material prosperity leads both to the misuse of available natural resources and to the exclusion of the weak and disadvantaged, either because they are differently abled (handicapped), or because they lack adequate information and technical expertise, or are incapable of decisive political action. Economic and social exclusion is a complete denial of human fraternity and a grave offense against human rights and the environment. The poorest are those who suffer most from such offenses, for three serious reasons: they are cast off by society, forced to live off what is discarded, and suffer unjustly from the abuse of the environment. They are part of today's widespread and quietly growing "culture of waste."

The dramatic reality of this whole situation of exclusion and inequality, with its evident effects, has led me, in union with the entire Christian people and many others, to take stock of my grave responsibility in this regard and to speak out, together with all those who are seeking urgently needed and effective solutions.

ADDRESS TO THE GENERAL ASSEMBLY OF THE UNITED NATIONS, UNITED NATIONS HEADQUARTERS, NEW YORK FRIDAY, SEPTEMBER 25, 2015

THE PLANET BELONGS TO ALL

With due respect for the autonomy and culture of every nation, we must never forget that the planet belongs to all mankind and is meant for all mankind; the mere fact that some people are born in places with fewer resources or less development does not justify the fact that they are living with less dignity. It must be reiterated that "the more fortunate should renounce some of their rights so as to place their goods more generously at the service of others" (Paul VI, *Octogesima Adveniens*).

APOSTOLIC EXHORTATION, *EVANGELII GAUDIUM*, 190
SUNDAY, NOVEMBER 24, 2013

Pope Francis @Pontifex · July 25, 2013

The measure of the greatness of a society is found in the way it treats those most in need, those who have nothing apart from their poverty.

A NEW KIND OF COOPERATION

How long will we continue to defend systems of production and consumption which exclude most of the world's population even from the crumbs which fall from the tables of the rich? The time has come to think and decide, beginning with each person and community rather than from market trends. Therefore, there must also be a change in the concept of work, goals and economic activity, food production and environmental protection. This is perhaps the only possibility for building an authentic future of peace, which today is also threatened by food insecurity.

This approach, which allows us to glimpse a new kind of cooperation, must involve and be of interest to States, international institutions and organizations of civil society, as well as communities of believers that, with their many works, live together with the least and share the same situations and needs, frustrations and hopes.

MESSAGE OF POPE FRANCIS FOR WORLD FOOD DAY 2014,
FROM THE VATICAN
THURSDAY, OCTOBER 16, 2014

THE DISGRACE OF WORLD HUNGER

It is a truly pressing duty to use the earth's resources in such a way that all may be free from hunger. Initiatives and possible solutions are many, and are not limited to an increase in production. It is well known that present production is sufficient, and yet millions of persons continue to suffer and die from hunger, and this is a real scandal. We need, then, to find ways by which all may benefit from the fruits of the earth, not only to avoid the widening gap between those who have more and those who must be content with the crumbs, but above all because it is a question of justice, equality and respect for every human being.

MESSAGE FOR THE 2014 WORLD DAY OF PEACE,
FROM THE VATICAN
SUNDAY, DECEMBER 8, 2013

Pope Francis @Pontifex · June 18, 2015
A decrease in the pace of production and consumption can at times give rise to another form of progress and development.

TRULY MUCH CAN BE DONE!

There are no uniform recipes, because each country or region has its own problems and limitations. It is also true that political realism may call for transitional measures and technologies, so long as these are accompanied by the gradual framing and acceptance of binding commitments. At the same time, on the national and local levels, much still needs to be done, such as promoting ways of conserving energy. These would include favoring forms of industrial production with maximum energy efficiency and diminished use of raw materials, removing from the market products which are less energy efficient or more polluting, improving transport systems, and encouraging the construction and repair of buildings aimed at reducing their energy consumption and levels of pollution. Political activity on the local level could also be directed to modifying consumption, developing an economy of waste disposal and recycling, protecting certain species and planning a diversified agriculture and the rotation of crops. Agriculture in poorer regions can be improved through investment in rural infrastructures, a better organization of local or national markets, systems of irrigation, and the development of techniques of sustainable agriculture. New forms of cooperation and community organization can be encouraged in order to defend the interests of small producers and preserve local ecosystems from destruction. Truly, much can be done!

ENCYCLICAL LETTER, *LAUDATO SI'*, 180
SUNDAY, MAY 24, 2015

Pope Francis @Pontifex · June 18, 2015
To blame population growth, and not an extreme consumerism on the part of some, is one way of refusing to face the issues.

IN HARMONY WITH NATURE

A just economy must create the conditions for everyone to be able to enjoy a childhood without want, to develop their talents when young, to work with full rights during their active years and to enjoy a dignified retirement as they grow older. It is an economy where human beings, in harmony with nature, structure the entire system of production and distribution in such a way that the abilities and needs of each individual find suitable expression in social life. You, and other peoples as well, sum up this desire in a simple and beautiful expression: "to live well," which is not the same as "to have a good time."

ADDRESS, WORLD MEETING OF POPULAR MOVEMENTS,
SANTA CRUZ DE LA SIERRA (BOLIVIA)
THURSDAY, JULY 9, 2015

Pope Francis @Pontifex · June 18, 2015
Scientific and technological progress cannot be equated with the progress of humanity and history.

DIRECTED TO THE COMMON GOOD

Politics and the economy tend to blame each other when it comes to poverty and environmental degradation. It is to be hoped that they can acknowledge their own mistakes and find forms of interaction directed to the common good. While some are concerned only with financial gain and others with holding on to or increasing their power, what we are left with are conflicts or spurious agreements where the last thing either party is concerned about is caring for the environment and protecting those who are most vulnerable.

ENCYCLICAL LETTER, *LAUDATO SI'*, 198
SUNDAY, MAY 24, 2015

A MORAL OBLIGATION

Working for a just distribution of the fruits of the earth and human labor is not mere philanthropy. It is a moral obligation. For Christians, the responsibility is even greater: it is a commandment. It is about giving to the poor and to peoples what is theirs by right. The universal destination of goods is not a figure of speech found in the Church's social teaching. It is a reality prior to private property. Property, especially when it affects natural resources, must always serve the needs of peoples.

ADDRESS, WORLD MEETING OF POPULAR MOVEMENTS,
SANTA CRUZ DE LA SIERRA (BOLIVIA)
THURSDAY, JULY 9, 2015

Pope Francis @Pontifex · March 24, 2013

We must not believe the Evil One when he tells us that there is nothing we can do in the face of violence, injustice and sin.

WE ARE AT A BREAKING POINT

On many concrete questions, the Church has no reason to offer a definitive opinion; she knows that honest debate must be encouraged among experts, while respecting divergent views. But we need only take a frank look at the facts to see that our common home is falling into serious disrepair. Hope would have us recognize that there is always a way out, that we can always redirect our steps, that we can always do something to solve our problems. Still, we can see signs that things are now reaching a breaking point, due to the rapid pace of change and degradation; these are evident in large-scale natural disasters as well as social and even financial crises, for the world's problems cannot be analyzed or explained in isolation.

ENCYCLICAL LETTER, *LAUDATO SI'*, 61
SUNDAY, MAY 24, 2015

THE REAL PROBLEM IS PEOPLE

Today it is said that many things cannot be done because there is not enough money. Yet there is always money to do some things and not enough to do others. For example, money is found to buy arms, to wage war, for unscrupulous financial transactions. This is usually kept quiet, what is frequently highlighted is that there is not enough money to create jobs, to invest in awareness, in talents, to plan new welfare, to safeguard the environment. The real problem is not money but people: we cannot ask of money what only people can do or create. Money alone does not create development, creating development takes people who have the courage to take the initiative.

VIDEO MESSAGE FOR THE FESTIVAL OF THE SOCIAL
DOCTRINE OF THE CHURCH, FROM THE VATICAN
THURSDAY, NOVEMBER 20, 2014

Pope Francis @Pontifex · June 18, 2015

Many things have to change course, but it is we human beings above all who need to change.

SOME ADVANCES HAVE BEEN MADE

In some countries, there are positive examples of environmental improvement: rivers, polluted for decades, have been cleaned up; native woodlands have been restored; landscapes have been beautified thanks to environmental renewal projects; beautiful buildings have been erected; advances have been made in the production of nonpolluting energy and in the improvement of public transportation. These achievements do not solve global problems, but they do show that men and women are still capable of intervening positively. For all our limitations, gestures of generosity, solidarity and care cannot but well up within us, since we were made for love.

ENCYCLICAL LETTER, *LAUDATO SI'*, 58
SUNDAY, MAY 24, 2015

Pope Francis @Pontifex · October 13, 2015
Let us learn solidarity. Without solidarity, our faith is dead.

SAY NO TO ALL FORMS OF COLONIALISM

Every significant action carried out in one part of the planet has universal, ecological, social and cultural repercussions. Even crime and violence have become globalized. Consequently, no government can act independently of a common responsibility. If we truly desire positive change, we have to humbly accept our interdependence, that is to say, our healthy interdependence. Interaction, however, is not the same as imposition; it is not the subordination of some to serve the interests of others. Colonialism, both old and new, which reduces poor countries to mere providers of raw material and cheap labor, engenders violence, poverty, forced migrations and all the evils which go hand in hand with these, precisely because, by placing the periphery at the service of the center, it denies those countries the right to an integral development. That is inequality, brothers and sisters, and inequality generates a violence which no police, military, or intelligence resources can control.

Let us say NO, then, to forms of colonialism old and new. Let us say YES to the encounter between peoples and cultures. Blessed are the peacemakers.

ADDRESS, WORLD MEETING OF POPULAR MOVEMENTS,
SANTA CRUZ DE LA SIERRA (BOLIVIA)
THURSDAY, JULY 9, 2015

A DISTINCTIVE WAY OF THINKING

Ecological culture cannot be reduced to a series of urgent and partial responses to the immediate problems of pollution, environmental decay and the depletion of natural resources. There needs to be a distinctive way of looking at things, a way of thinking, policies, an educational program, a lifestyle and a spirituality which together generate resistance to the assault of the technocratic paradigm. Otherwise, even the best ecological initiatives can find themselves caught up in the same globalized logic. To seek only a technical remedy to each environmental problem which comes up is to separate what is in reality interconnected and to mask the true and deepest problems of the global system.

ENCYCLICAL LETTER, *LAUDATO SI'*, 111
SUNDAY, MAY 24, 2015

A JUST AND SUSTAINABLE DEVELOPMENT

In a world that tends to economic and cultural globalization, every effort must be made to ensure that growth and development are put at the service of all and not just limited parts of the population. Furthermore, such development will only be authentic if it is sustainable and just, that is, if it has the rights of the poor and respect for the environment close to heart. Alongside the globalization of the markets there must also be a corresponding globalization of solidarity; together with economic growth there must be a greater respect for creation.

ADDRESS TO CIVIL AUTHORITIES, PRESIDENTIAL PALACE, TIRANA (ALBANIA)
SUNDAY, SEPTEMBER 21, 2014

Pope Francis @Pontifex · June 18, 2015

At times more zeal is shown in protecting other species than in defending the equal dignity of human beings.

HONEST AND OPEN DEBATE

There are certain environmental issues where it is not easy to achieve a broad consensus. Here I would state once more that the Church does not presume to settle scientific questions or to replace politics. But I am concerned to encourage an honest and open debate so that particular interests or ideologies will not prejudice the common good.

ENCYCLICAL LETTER, *LAUDATO SI'*, 188
SUNDAY, MAY 24, 2015

Pope Francis @Pontifex · June 18, 2015
We need a new dialogue about how we are shaping the future of our planet. #LaudatoSi

RESIST THE ECONOMY OF EXCLUSION

In the case of global political and economic organization, much more needs to be achieved, since an important part of humanity does not share in the benefits of progress and is in fact relegated to the status of second-class citizens. Future sustainable development goals must therefore be formulated and carried out with generosity and courage, so that they can have a real impact on the structural causes of poverty and hunger, attain more substantial results in protecting the environment, ensure dignified and productive labor for all, and provide appropriate protection for the family, which is an essential element in sustainable human and social development. Specifically, this involves challenging all forms of injustice and resisting the "economy of exclusion," the "throwaway culture," and the "culture of death" which nowadays sadly risk becoming passively accepted.

ADDRESS TO THE UN SYSTEM CHIEF EXECUTIVES BOARD
FOR COORDINATION, CONSISTORY HALL
FRIDAY, MAY 9, 2014

CARE FOR INDIGENOUS COMMUNITIES

Many intensive forms of environmental exploitation and degradation not only exhaust the resources which provide local communities with their livelihood, but also undo the social structures which, for a long time, shaped cultural identity and their sense of the meaning of life and community. The disappearance of a culture can be just as serious, or even more serious, than the disappearance of a species of plant or animal. The imposition of a dominant lifestyle linked to a single form of production can be just as harmful as the altering of ecosystems.

In this sense, it is essential to show special care for indigenous communities and their cultural traditions. They are not merely one minority among others, but should be the principal dialogue partners, especially when large projects affecting their land are proposed. For them, land is not a commodity but rather a gift from God and from their ancestors who rest there, a sacred space with which they need to interact if they are to maintain their identity and values. When they remain on their land, they themselves care for it best.

ENCYCLICAL LETTER, *LAUDATO SI'*, 145–146
SUNDAY, MAY 24, 2015

OUR COMMON DESTINY

The notion of the common good also extends to future generations. The global economic crises have made painfully obvious the detrimental effects of disregarding our common destiny, which cannot exclude those who come after us. We can no longer speak of sustainable development apart from intergenerational solidarity. Once we start to think about the kind of world we are leaving to future generations, we look at things differently; we realize that the world is a gift which we have freely received and must share with others. Since the world has been given to us, we can no longer view reality in a purely utilitarian way, in which efficiency and productivity are entirely geared to our individual benefit. Intergenerational solidarity is not optional, but rather a basic question of justice, since the world we have received also belongs to those who will follow us.

ENCYCLICAL LETTER, *LAUDATO SI'*, 159
SUNDAY, MAY 24, 2015

WORKING FOR THE GLOBALIZATION OF SOLIDARITY

If we want to deliver to future generations an improved environmental, economic, cultural and social patrimony, which we inherited, we are called to assume the responsibility of working for the globalization of solidarity. Solidarity is a demand that that arises from the same network of interconnections which develop with globalization. The social doctrine of the Church teaches us that the principle of solidarity is implemented in harmony with that of subsidiarity. Thanks to the effect of these two principles, the processes are at the service of man, and justice is growing. Without justice there can be no true and lasting peace.

ADDRESS, WORLD CONGRESS OF ACCOUNTANTS,
PAUL VI AUDIENCE HALL
FRIDAY, NOVEMBER 14, 2014

Pope Francis @Pontifex · June 18, 2015
A true "ecological debt" exists, particularly between the global north and south.

STEWARD OF THE EARTH'S RICHES

The goods of the earth are meant for everyone, and however much someone may parade his property, which is legitimate, it has a social mortgage—always. In this way we move beyond purely economic justice, based on commerce, towards social justice, which upholds the fundamental human right to a dignified life. And, continuing with the theme of justice, the tapping of natural resources, which are so abundant in Ecuador, must not be concerned with short-term benefits. As stewards of these riches which we have received, we have an obligation towards society as a whole and towards future generations. We cannot bequeath this heritage to them without proper care for the environment, without a sense of gratuitousness born of our contemplation of the created world.... We received this world as an inheritance from past generations, but we must also remember that we received it as a loan from our children and from future generations, to whom we will have to return it! And we will have to return it in a better off state—that is gratuitousness!

ADDRESS TO POLITICAL, ECONOMIC AND CIVIC LEADERS,
SAN FRANCISCO CHURCH, QUITO (ECUADOR)
TUESDAY, JULY 7, 2015

AN ETHICAL IMPERATIVE TO ACT

The consequences of environmental changes, which are already being dramatically felt in many countries, especially the insular states of the Pacific, remind us of the gravity of neglect and inaction. The time to find global solutions is running out. We can find appropriate solutions only if we act together and in agreement. There is therefore a clear, definitive and urgent ethical imperative to act.

An effective fight against global warming will be possible only through a responsible collective action which overcomes particular interests and behaviors and develops unfettered by political and economic pressures. A collective response which is also capable of overcoming mistrust and of fostering a culture of solidarity, of encounter and of dialogue, capable of demonstrating responsibility to protect the planet and the human family.

MESSAGE FOR THE 20TH CONFERENCE OF THE
PARTIES TO THE UNITED NATIONS FRAMEWORK
CONVENTION ON CLIMATE CHANGE
(LIMA, PERU 1–12 DECEMBER 2014)
THURSDAY, NOVEMBER 27, 2014

REDUCING GREENHOUSE GASES

Reducing greenhouse gases requires honesty, courage and responsibility, above all on the part of those countries which are more powerful and pollute the most. The Conference of the United Nations on Sustainable Development, "Rio+20" (Rio de Janeiro 2012), issued a wide-ranging but ineffectual outcome document. International negotiations cannot make significant progress due to positions taken by countries which place their national interests above the global common good. Those who will have to suffer the consequences of what we are trying to hide will not forget this failure of conscience and responsibility. Even as this Encyclical was being prepared, the debate was intensifying. We believers cannot fail to ask God for a positive outcome to the present discussions so that future generations will not have to suffer the effects of our ill-advised delays.

ENCYCLICAL LETTER, *LAUDATO SI'*, 169
SUNDAY, MAY 24, 2015

Pope Francis @Pontifex · June 18, 2015

Reducing greenhouse gases requires honesty, courage and responsibility. #LaudatoSi

A CRITICAL MOMENT IN HISTORY

It seems clear to me also that climate change is a problem which can no longer be left to a future generation. When it comes to the care of our "common home," we are living at a critical moment of history.... To use a telling phrase of the Reverend Martin Luther King, we can say that we have defaulted on a promissory note and now is the time to honor it.

We know by faith that "the Creator does not abandon us; he never forsakes his loving plan or repents of having created us. Humanity still has the ability to work together in building our common home" (*Laudato Si'*, 13). As Christians inspired by this certainty, we wish to commit ourselves to the conscious and responsible care of our common home.

ADDRESS, WELCOMING CEREMONY, WHITE HOUSE,
WASHINGTON, D.C.
WEDNESDAY, SEPTEMBER 23, 2015

EMPOWERING INTERNATIONAL INSTITUTIONS

The same mindset which stands in the way of making radical decisions to reverse the trend of global warming also stands in the way of achieving the goal of eliminating poverty. A more responsible overall approach is needed to deal with both problems: the reduction of pollution and the development of poorer countries and regions. The twenty-first century, while maintaining systems of governance inherited from the past, is witnessing a weakening of the power of nation states, chiefly because the economic and financial sectors, being transnational, tends to prevail over the political. Given this situation, it is essential to devise stronger and more efficiently organized international institutions, with functionaries who are appointed fairly by agreement among national governments, and empowered to impose sanctions.

ENCYCLICAL LETTER, *LAUDATO SI'*, 175
SUNDAY, MAY 24, 2015

Pope Francis @Pontifex · June 18, 2015
A fragile world challenges us to devise intelligent ways of directing, developing and limiting our power.

CARING FOR OUR ECOSYSTEMS

Caring for ecosystems demands farsightedness, since no one looking for quick and easy profit is truly interested in their preservation. But the cost of the damage caused by such selfish lack of concern is much greater than the economic benefits to be obtained. Where certain species are destroyed or seriously harmed, the values involved are incalculable. We can be silent witnesses to terrible injustices if we think that we can obtain significant benefits by making the rest of humanity, present and future, pay the extremely high costs of environmental deterioration.

ENCYCLICAL LETTER, *LAUDATO SI'*, 36
SUNDAY, MAY 24, 2015

Pope Francis @Pontifex · June 19 2014
There is never a reason to lose hope. Jesus says: "I am with you until the end of the world."

AN EDUCATIONAL CHALLENGE

An awareness of the gravity of today's cultural and ecological crisis must be translated into new habits. Many people know that our current progress and the mere amassing of things and pleasures are not enough to give meaning and joy to the human heart, yet they feel unable to give up what the market sets before them. In those countries which should be making the greatest changes in consumer habits, young people have a new ecological sensitivity and a generous spirit, and some of them are making admirable efforts to protect the environment. At the same time, they have grown up in a milieu of extreme consumerism and affluence which makes it difficult to develop other habits. We are faced with an educational challenge.

Environmental education has broadened its goals. Whereas in the beginning it was mainly centered on scientific information, consciousness-raising and the prevention of environmental risks, it tends now to include a critique of the "myths" of a modernity grounded in a utilitarian mindset (individualism, unlimited progress, competition, consumerism, the unregulated market). It seeks also to restore the various levels of ecological equilibrium, establishing harmony within ourselves, with others, with nature and other living creatures, and with God. Environmental education should facilitate making the leap towards the transcendent which gives ecological ethics its deepest meaning.

ENCYCLICAL LETTER, *LAUDATO SI'*, 209–210
SUNDAY, MAY 24, 2015

A PRAYER INTENTION

Believers and unbelievers agree that the earth is our common heritage, the fruits of which should benefit everyone. However, what is happening in the world we live in?

The relationship between poverty and the fragility of the planet requires another way of managing the economy and measuring progress, conceiving a new way of living, because we need a change that unites us all, free from the slavery of consumerism.

This month I make a special request: That we may take good care of creation—a gift freely given—cultivating and protecting it for future generations, caring for our common home.

UNIVERSAL PRAYER INTENTION FOR THE MONTH OF
FEBRUARY 2016, FROM THE VATICAN

Pope Francis @Pontifex · May 19, 2014

The Holy Spirit transforms and renews us, creates harmony and unity, and gives us courage and joy for our mission.

THE URGENT CHALLENGE OF PROTECTING OUR HOME

What kind of world do we want to leave to our children (cf. *Laudato Si'*, 160)? We cannot answer these questions alone, by ourselves. It is the Spirit who challenges us to respond as part of the great human family. Our common house can no longer tolerate sterile divisions. The urgent challenge of protecting our home includes the effort to bring the entire human family together in the pursuit of a sustainable and integral development, for we know that things can change (cf. *Laudato Si'*, 13). May our children find in us models and incentives to communion, not division! May our children find in us men and women capable of joining others in bringing to full flower all the good seeds which the Father has sown!

HOMILY, 8TH WORLD MEETING OF FAMILIES, BENJAMIN
FRANKLIN PARKWAY, PHILADELPHIA
SUNDAY, SEPTEMBER 27, 2015

THE JOY OF OUR HOPE

At the end, we will find ourselves face to face with the infinite beauty of God (cf. 1 Corinthians 13:12), and be able to read with admiration and happiness the mystery of the universe, which with us will share in unending plenitude. Even now we are journeying towards the sabbath of eternity, the new Jerusalem, towards our common home in heaven. Jesus says: "I make all things new" (Revelations 21:5). Eternal life will be a shared experience of awe, in which each creature, resplendently transfigured, will take its rightful place and have something to give those poor men and women who will have been liberated once and for all.

In the meantime, we come together to take charge of this home which has been entrusted to us, knowing that all the good which exists here will be taken up into the heavenly feast. In union with all creatures, we journey through this land seeking God.... Let us sing as we go. May our struggles and our concern for this planet never take away the joy of our hope.

ENCYCLICAL LETTER, *LAUDATO SI'*, 243–244
SUNDAY, MAY 24, 2015

Pope Francis @Pontifex · June 19, 2015

Let us sing as we go. May our struggles and our concern for this planet never take away the joy of our hope.

PRAISE BE TO GOD!

God, who calls us to generous commitment and to give him our all, offers us the light and the strength needed to continue on our way. In the heart of this world, the Lord of life, who loves us so much, is always present. He does not abandon us, he does not leave us alone, for he has united himself definitively to our earth, and his love constantly impels us to find new ways forward. Praise be to him!

ENCYCLICAL LETTER, *LAUDATO SI'*, 245
SUNDAY, MAY 24, 2015

APPENDICES

Sharing the concern of my beloved brother, Ecumenical Patriarch Bartholomew, for the future of creation (cf. *Laudato Si'*, 7–9), and at the suggestion of his representative, Metropolitan Ioannis of Pergamum, who took part in the presentation of the Encyclical *Laudato Si'* on care for our common home, I wish to inform you that I have decided to institute in the Catholic Church the "World Day of Prayer for the Care of Creation" which, beginning this year, is to be celebrated on 1 September, as has been the custom in the Orthodox Church for some time.

As Christians we wish to contribute to resolving the ecological crisis which humanity is presently experiencing. In doing so, we must first rediscover in our own rich spiritual patrimony the deepest motivations for our concern for the care of creation. We need always to keep in mind that, for believers in Jesus Christ, the Word of God who became man for our sake, "the life of the spirit is not dissociated from the body or from nature or from worldly realities, but lived in and with them, in communion with all that surrounds us" (*Laudato Si'*, 216). The ecological crisis thus summons us to a profound spiritual conversion: Christians are called to "an ecological conversion whereby the effects of their encounter with Jesus Christ become evident in their relationship with the world around them" (*Laudato Si'*, 217). For "living our vocation to be protectors of God's handiwork is essential to a life of virtue; it is not an optional or a secondary aspect of our Christian experience" (*Laudato Si'*, 217).

The annual World Day of Prayer for the Care of Creation will offer individual believers and communities a fitting opportunity to reaffirm their personal vocation to be stewards of creation, to thank God for the wonderful handiwork which he has entrusted to our care, and to implore his help for the protection of creation as well as his pardon for the sins committed against the world in which we live. The celebration of this day, on the same date as the Orthodox Church, will be a valuable opportunity to bear witness to our growing communion with our Orthodox brothers and sisters. We live at a time when all Christians are faced with the same decisive challenges, to which we must respond together, in order to be more credible and effective. It is my hope that this day will in some way also involve other Churches and ecclesial communities, and be celebrated in union with similar initiatives of the World Council of Churches.

I ask you, Cardinal Turkson, as President of the Pontifical Council for Justice and Peace, to inform the Justice and Peace Commissions of the Bishops' Conferences, as well as the national and international organizations involved in environmental issues, of the establishment of the World Day of Prayer for the Care of Creation, so that, with due regard for local needs and situations, it can be properly celebrated with the participation of the entire People of God: priests, men and women religious and the lay faithful. For this reason, it will be the task of your Council, in cooperation with the various Episcopal Conferences, to arrange suitable ways of publicizing and celebrating the day, so that this annual event will become a significant occasion for prayer, reflection, conversion and the adoption of appropriate lifestyles.

I ask you, Cardinal Koch, as President of the Pontifical Council for the Promotion of Christian Unity, to make the necessary contacts with the Ecumenical Patriarchate and with other ecumenical organizations so that this World Day can serve as a sign of a common journey in which all believers in Christ take part. It will also be your Council's responsibility to ensure that it is coordinated with similar initiatives undertaken by the World Council of Churches.

In expressing my hope that, as a result of wide cooperation, the World Day of Prayer for the Care of Creation will be inaugurated and develop in the best way possible, I invoke upon this initiative the intercession of Mary, Mother of God, and of Saint Francis of Assisi, whose Canticle of the Creatures inspires so many men and women of goodwill to live in praise of the Creator and with respect for creation. As a pledge of spiritual fruitfulness, I impart my Apostolic Blessing to you, Eminent Brothers, and to all those who share in your ministry.

From the Vatican, Thursday, August 6, 2015

Feast of the Transfiguration of the Lord

Prayers for Our Earth

Publisher's Note: At the conclusion of Laudato Si', *Pope Francis offers two prayers, "A Prayer for Our Earth" and "A Christian Prayer in Union with Creation." He writes, "The first we can share with all who believe in a God who is the all-powerful Creator, while in the other we Christians ask for inspiration to take up the commitment to creation set before us by the Gospel of Jesus."*

A Prayer for Our Earth

All-powerful God, you are present in the whole universe
and in the smallest of your creatures.
You embrace with your tenderness all that exists.
Pour out upon us the power of your love,
that we may protect life and beauty.
Fill us with peace, that we may live
as brothers and sisters, harming no one.

O God of the poor,
help us to rescue the abandoned and forgotten of this earth,
so precious in your eyes.

Bring healing to our lives,
that we may protect the world and not prey on it,
that we may sow beauty, not pollution and destruction.

Touch the hearts
of those who look only for gain
at the expense of the poor and the earth.
Teach us to discover the worth of each thing,
to be filled with awe and contemplation,
to recognize that we are profoundly united
with every creature
as we journey towards your infinite light.
We thank you for being with us each day.
Encourage us, we pray, in our struggle
for justice, love and peace.

A Christian Prayer in Union with Creation

Father, we praise you with all your creatures.
They came forth from your all-powerful hand;
they are yours, filled with your presence and your tender
  love.
Praise be to you!

Son of God, Jesus,
through you all things were made.
You were formed in the womb of Mary our Mother,
you became part of this earth,
and you gazed upon this world with human eyes.

Today you are alive in every creature
in your risen glory.
Praise be to you!

Holy Spirit, by your light
you guide this world towards the Father's love
and accompany creation as it groans in travail.
You also dwell in our hearts
and you inspire us to do what is good.
Praise be to you!

Triune Lord, wondrous community of infinite love,
teach us to contemplate you
in the beauty of the universe,
for all things speak of you.
Awaken our praise and thankfulness
for every being that you have made.
Give us the grace to feel profoundly joined
to everything that is.

God of love, show us our place in this world
as channels of your love
for all the creatures of this earth,
for not one of them is forgotten in your sight.
Enlighten those who possess power and money
that they may avoid the sin of indifference,

that they may love the common good, advance the weak,
and care for this world in which we live.
The poor and the earth are crying out.
O Lord, seize us with your power and light,
help us to protect all life,
to prepare for a better future,
for the coming of your Kingdom
of justice, peace, love and beauty.
Praise be to you!
Amen.